REBELLIOUS DAUGHTERS OF HISTORY
+ OTHER POSTS FROM THE LOCKDOWN 2020

JUDY COX
REBELLIOUS DAUGHTERS OF HISTORY

a Redwords book

REDWORDS

Rebelious Doaughters of History
by Judy Cox
First published by Redwords, January 2021

All entries first posted on Facebook during Covid-19
lockdown 2020

Set in ITC Franklin Gothic and Georgia
Design and production Roger Huddle
Printed by Halstan Press, Amersham HP6 6HJ

Paperback: 978-1-912926-94-7
Kindle: 978-1-912926-95-4
e-pub: 978-1-912926-96-1

Redwords is linked to Bookmarks: the socialist bookshop
1 Bloomsbury Street, London WC1B 3QE

bookmarksbookshop.co.uk

Contents

✪Massive thanks to all those who engaged with these posts and encouraged me to keep going, especially Ali Brown, Kate Meyer, Sam Kirk, Laura Hayes, Caroline Conway, Fatima Uygun and Jeannie Robinson. Special thanks to Roger Huddle, Rob Hoveman, Elisa, Peter and Fred Cox.

★ The Rebellious Daughters are women drawn from across continents and decades connected by their determination to challenge prejudice, inequality and injustice. From Black Panthers to Victorian trade unionists, from slave insurgents to radical poets, the Rebellious Daughters all defied the system and many won. This project began as a response to lockdown. In daily Facebook posts I drew attention to how women of the past had fought back. The only criterion was that the women looked to militant collective action rather than Parliament or Congress. I also chose women whose lives were unconventional, those who challenged expectations by speaking out and finding their own ways to love as they were fighting for a radical transformation of their world. The posts resonated with readers struggling to deal with the Covid 19 threat. Hundreds of people responded with positive comments and suggestions and many urged me to turn the posts into a book. The first Daughters were drawn from my doctoral research on radical women of the nineteenth century.

As lockdown continued, I researched unfamiliar Rebellious Daughters in response to shifting political moments – clapping for carers, Black Lives Matter and strike movements are all reflected in the Rebellious Daughters.

Readers turned into contributors and new voices put forward their own choices. Many of the Rebellious Daughters are women you will be surprised you never heard of before. The book introduces women in accessible mini-biographies and excavates their lives from the obscurity to which they have been condemned by a historiography which is misogynistic, racist and centred on men in positions of power. *Rebellious Daughters* creates a vivid and inspiring series of portraits of women who refused to stay in their place in the expectation that their example would strengthen women fighting for a better world

Soldaderas: women fighters of the Mexican Revolution.

29 March
Breaking new ground: Frances Wright (1795-1852)

Wright was a Scottish born lecturer, writer, freethinker, feminist and Abolitionist. She mixed on equal terms with radical thinkers and philosophers in Britain and the US. In 1825, she became the only woman to set up a utopian socialist community, the Nashoba Commune, Tennessee. It was the only such community to welcome freed slaves as members and caused a scandal by permitting interracial relationships. In the late 1820s, Wright was the first woman to give public lectures to mixed audiences. Thousands heard her demand radical reforms, such as universal education, abolition of slavery, birth control and sexual freedom for women. She denounced organised religion and was a passionate opponent of capital punishment. Wright was vilified by the church and the press and frequently attacked by violent mobs.

Unlike other feminists of the time, such as Mary Wollstonecraft, Frances supported working class organisation. She was a prominent supporter of the working men's associations which sprang up in New York in the late 1820s.

Frances wrote plays, published editions of her lectures and became the first woman to edit a newspaper in the US, first the *Free Enquirer* and, later, *The Sentinel* and *Working Man's Advocate*. A Chartist wrote the first biography of Wright, and the Chartist newspaper, the *Northern Star* advertised all her works, including her last work, the polemical political history, *England, the Civiliser*, which savaged Whig ideas of historical progress. In 1831, Frances married Guillaume D'Arusmont, who had taught at Nashoba, and had a daughter, Sylvia. When Wright divorced D'Arusmont in 1850, she had to fight for custody and control of her personal wealth. The case was unresolved when she died two years later, aged 57.

Poem:
Elizabeth Barrett Browning: Case Guidi Windows(1848)

Elizabeth Barrett Browning was one of the most prolific and successful writers of the Victorian era. An admirer of Mary Wollstonecraft, she wrote about oppression, industrialization and politics. Elizabeth Barrett eloped with Robert Browning and was living in Florence in 1848, where she witnessed an uprising against Church and Empire. She wrote a book of poems, *Case Guidi Windows*, to win support for the cause of Italian unification and democracy. In the poem, Elizabeth describes the revolt against Duke Leopold II, and her words captured the heightened sense of political engagement among the people of insurgent Florence:

Long live the people! How they lived! And boiled
And bubbled in the cauldron of the street!
How the young blustered, nor the old recoiled,
And what a thunderous stir of tongues and feet
Trod flat the palpitating bells and foiled
The joyguns of their echo, shattering it!
How they pulled down the Duke's arms everywhere!
How they set up new café signs, to show
Where patriots might sup ices in pure air
(Yet the fresh paint smelt somewhat). To and fro
How marched the civic guard, and stopped to stare
When boys broke windows in a civic glow.
How rebel songs were sung to loyal tunes,
And the pope cursed, in ecclesiastic metres!

30 March
Locked up but never silenced: Jeanne Deroin (1805-1894)

Jeanne Deroin was one of the great women revolutionaries of the nineteenth century. Born in Paris in 1805, Deroin scraped a living as a seamstress to support her alcoholic husband and four children, one of whom was severely disabled. She became a utopian socialist, committed to the abolition of private property, the replacement of competition with cooperation and gender equality. Jeanne wrote to her English comrade Anne Knight explaining she was seeking, 'the complete, radical abolition of all the privileges of sex, of race, of birth, of rank, and of fortune'.

During the French Revolution of 1848, she organised women workers and set up a socialist paper aimed at women and sold on the streets. The *Voice des Femmes* demanded the right for women to work and to vote. Jeanne fiercely opposed the misogyny of radical men like Joseph Proudhon and she became the first woman to attempt to stand for parliament. She was arrested in 1851 with her comrade Pauline Roland, but they continued to agitate from their prison cells. Jeanne and Pauline wrote to the American Women's Rights Convention of 1852: 'Sisters of America! Your socialist sisters of France are united with you in the vindication of the right of woman to civil and political equality. We have, moreover, the profound conviction that only by the power of association based on solidarity – by the union of the working classes of both sexes to organize labour – can be acquired, completely and particularly, the civil and political equality of woman, and the social right of all'.

On her release, Jeanne fled to London, where

she joined the First International, alongside Karl Marx and Frederick Engels, and later she joined the Socialist League alongside Eleanor Marx and William Morris. When she died in 1894, the local paper reported on her funeral: 'The remains of Mdme Jeanne Deroin, the lady who obtained considerable notoriety during the French Revolution of 1848, were laid to rest in Hammersmith Cemetery on Saturday afternoon. There was a large attendance of sympathising friends, including a contingent of local Socialists, who attended the funeral, headed by their banner. Mr. William Morris, Mr. Sparling, and other wellknown holders of advanced ideas spoke at the grave side. At the conclusion of the ceremony, one of Mr. W. Morris's Chants for Socialists entitled "No Master" was sung'.

Jeanne Deroin sits in front of William Morris, who is the man with the long white beard.

31 March
From suffrage to communism: Adelaide Knight (1871-1950)

Adelaide Knight was born in 1871 and lived with her working-class family on Kenilworth Road in Bethnal Green. After a childhood injury she used crutches or a stick to help her walk for the rest of her life.

In 1894 Adelaide married a sailor, Donald Adolphus Brown, who was born in what is now Guyana. He shared Adelaide's political beliefs and supported her activism. They both joined the Independent Labour Party and Donald took Adelaide's surname and was widely known as Donald Knight.

When the first London branch of the Women's Social and Political Union (WSPU) was opened in Canning Town in 1906, Adelaide was its secretary.

In June 1906 she was arrested alongside Annie Kenney and Mrs Sparborough when they tried to see the prime minister, Herbert Asquith.

The women were sentenced to prison for six weeks unless they agreed to be bound over for one year and give up their campaigning. It was a difficult decision for Adelaide as she was in poor health, and had two small children to care for, but all three women chose prison. Adelaide said: 'I refuse to barter my freedom to act according to my conscience, while my health permits me to fight on'. She sang 'The Red Flag' every morning to keep her spirits up.

Adelaide left the WSPU and joined Sylvia Pankhurst in the militant East London Suffrage Federation, which campaigned with and for working-class women. They linked suffrage to economic reform, opposed the First World War and celebrated the Russian Revolution. In 1920 Adelaide and Sylvia and several other women from the East End suffrage movement became founding members of the Communist Party of Great Britain.

Poem:
Sylvia Pankhurst: Writ On Cold Slate (1921)

 Sylvia Pankhurst was one of the great woman suffrage campaigners and revolutionary socialists. She was arrested multiple times during her fight for the right to vote. She also published a collection of poetry called *Writ on Cold Slate*. The title, and this poem, come from the fact that she was not allowed pencil, pen or paper whilst in prison and could only write on a slate with chalk.

Writ on Cold Slate

Whilst many a poet to his love hath writ,
boasting that thus he gave immortal life,
my faithful lines upon inconstant slate,
destined to swift execution reach not thee.

In other ages dungeons might be strange,
with ancient mouldiness their airs infect,
but kindly warders would the tablets bring,
so captives might their precious thoughts inscribing,
the treasures of the fruitful mind preserve,
and culling thus its flowers, postpone decay.

Only this age that loudly boasts Reform,
hath set its seal of vengeance 'gainst the mind,
decreeing thought in prison shall be writ,
save on cold slate and swiftly washed away.

1 April
The intransigent Communard: Natalie Lemel (1827-1922)

Natalie Lemel was a Parisian radical bookbinder. In the 1860s she became one of very few female strike leaders and campaigned for equal pay for women. She joined the First International in 1865.

In 1871, Natalie became a leading figure in the Paris Commune. She joined with other members of the First International including Elizabeth Dimitrieff to establish the 'Union of Women' to campaign for support for the Commune among working women. Every member of the Union was a member of the First International. The Union campaigned for equal pay, for education for girls, for the right to divorce and for work. It became one of the most powerful organisations of the Commune. When the Commune came under attack, Lemel issued a defiant  public address: 'We have come to the supreme moment, when we must be able to die for our Nation. No more weakness! No more uncertainty! All women to arms! All women to duty! Versailles must be wiped out!'

Natalie was one of many women who fought on the barricades of Paris. After the defeat of the Commune, Lemel was sentenced to exile in the Canadian Nouvelle-Calédonie penal colony. She shared a cell with another great female Communard, Louise Michel. Natalie had to wait for an amnesty declared in 1880, before she could return to Paris. Unbowed by these experiences, Lemel worked for a radical paper, *L'Intransigant,* and continued her fight for women's rights. She died in 1922.

Poem:
Percy Bysshe Shelley: Ozymandias (1818)

⭐ 'Shelley was persecuted by the problem of communication. He was not, as his worshippers in later decades pretended, a 'lyric' poet interested only in writing beautiful poetry. He was a man with revolutionary ideas, and he wanted to transmit them.

Shelley wanted the truth about repression and exploitation to go ringing through each heart and brain, so that each heart and brain would unite in action to end that repression and exploitation. So, particularly in his later poems, he concentrated all his mastery of language, all his genius with rhyme and rhythm into translating the ideas of the revolution to the masses.

He survives for us not as a lyric poet but as one of the most eloquent agitators of all time.' (Paul Foot)

Ozymandias

I met a traveller from an antique land
Who said: "Two vast and trunkless legs of stone
Stand in the desert . . . Near them, on the sand,
Half sunk, a shattered visage lies, whose frown,
And wrinkled lip, and sneer of cold command,
Tell that its sculptor well those passions read
Which yet survive, stamped on these lifeless things,
The hand that mocked them, and the heart that fed:
And on the pedestal these words appear:
'My name is Ozymandias, king of kings:
Look on my works, ye Mighty, and despair!'
Nothing beside remains. Round the decay
Of that colossal wreck, boundless and bare
The lone and level sands stretch far away.

2 April
Liberator, soldier and suffragist: Harriet Tubman (1822-1913)

Harriet Tubman was one of the greatest women to fight against slavery and women's oppression. She will be familiar to many as a leader of the underground railway but this was only one chapter in her remarkable life.

Harriet was born a slave. She struggled with the effects of a head injury inflicted by a slave owner, she never learnt to read or write and spent her whole life in poverty.

Harriet was the most famous conductor of the Underground Railroad. In a decade she guided 100s of slaves to freedom. She also built a network of supporters. Tubman met the abolitionist John Brown in 1858, and helped him plan and recruit supporters for his 1859 raid on Harpers Ferry. During the American Civil War, in 1861 Tubman volunteered to join the Massachusetts troop, the only African-American among the white troops stationed at Fort Monroe. The fort was flooded with fugitives. Tubman worked as a nurse, cook and laundress. In 1862 Tubman travelled to South Carolina to a hospital at Port Royal. Injured Soldiers were dying of illnesses like typhoid, cholera, malaria, yellow fever, chicken pox and dysentery. Tubman was knowledgeable in local roots to treat diseases; her healing powers became legendary among soldiers.

After the Emancipation Proclamation in 1863, black people were allowed to enrol in the military. Tubman lead a group of scouts to create lifelines and escape routes for trapped slaves. On the night of 2 June 1863 Tubman guided a troop of 150 black soldiers of the Second South Carolina battalion on the Combahee River. The plan was to liberate as many slaves by catching slaveholders by surprise. The attack became known as the Combahee River Raid and liberated more than 750 slaves. The first black feminists to develop intersectionality theory in the 1970s called themselves the Commager River Collective in memory of Tubman.

When the war was over in 1865 Harriet returned home to New York. A battle to get compensation for her services would last thirty years. Tubman joined the campaign for women's right to vote. She toured New York, Boston and Washington

arguing for women's suffrage rights. She was especially interested in the rights of African-American women. In 1896, she was the key speaker at the first meeting of the National Association of Afro-American women. She established the Harriet Tubman Home for the Elderly in 1908.

Harriet Tubman Statue at the Equal Rights Heritage Center, Auburn NYS

3 April
'Heroine of the Bolsheviki': Alexandra Kollontai (1872-1952)

Alexandra Kollontai was a leading figure in the international socialist movement and the most prominent female Bolshevik during the Russian Revolution of 1917. Born into aristocratic privilege, the Finnish-Russian, Alexandra married in 1893 and had a son, Mikhail, the following year. Alexandra joined the revolutionary underground movements. She witnessed the atrocities which sparked the 1905 Revolution. She was a member of the Mensheviks but responded to the horrors of the First World War by joining Lenin and the Bolsheviks. She was one of the Party's most powerful speakers and a tireless activist, finding new ways to reach out to working-class women. Alexandra was the only leading member of the Petrograd Bolsheviks who supported Lenin's calls for revolution in October 1917.

In 1918, the American periodical *Current Opinion* called her the 'Heroine of the Bolsheviki upheaval in Petrograd' and announced its incredulous readers that 'she holds a cabinet portfolio, dresses like a Parisian, and does not believe in marriage'. Alexandra made an enormous contribution to the Marxist literature on women's oppression, such as *The Social Basis of the Woman Question* and *Communism and the Family*.

After the October Revolution, she helped to set up the Zhenotdel (the women's section of the Party). She oversaw a wide variety of legal reforms and public policies aimed at introducing full equality for working women. She also created socialised provision of catering, cleaning and childcare to liberate working women and to create the basis of an emancipated sexual morality. When Stalin overthrew the Revolutionary regime, she initially tried to oppose him. Alexandra was sent off to Norway to serve as ambassador. She died in 1952, in Moscow, one of a tiny handful of old Bolsheviks to survive Stalin's purges.

4 April
Perfect freedom and equality: Anna Wheeler (1780-1848)

Anna Wheeler was one of the first socialist feminists to speak out in public and demand radical reform. Anna married Francis Wheeler when she was fifteen. He was an abusive alcoholic and she later left him. Anna was left penniless when he died in 1820. She supported herself and her children by translating the works of French socialists into English.

In London, she met Robert Owen, Jeremy Bentham and Frances Wright, and became close friends with radical William Thompson. In 1825, they wrote *An Appeal of One Half of the Human Race, Women, Against the Pretensions of the Other Half, Men, to Retain them in Political, and Hence in Civil and Domestic, Slavery.*

In the Preface, William addressed Anna: 'You look forward, as I do, to a state of society very different from that which now exists, in which effort of all is to out wit, supplant, and snatch from each other; where the so called system of morals is little more than a mass of hypocrisy preached by knaves, and practised by them, to keep their slaves, male as well as female, in blind uninquiring obedience; and where the whole motley fabric is kept together by fear and blood. You look forward to a better aspect of society; where the principle of benevolence shall supersede that of fear; where restless and anxious individual competition shall give place to mutual co-operation...' In an address of 1829, Anna encouraged women to create an organisation, 'to obtain... the removal of the disabilities of women and the introduction of a system of equal education for the Infants of both sexes'.

Wheeler was a friend of the French feminists and socialists Flora Tristan, Jeanne Deroin, Charles Fourier and Henry Saint-Simon. In the early 1830s. she helped to establish the journal '*Tribune des Femmes*'. Anna Wheeler died in 1848.

5 April
'Bury me in a Free Land' Frances Harper (1825-1911)

Frances Harper, born in 1825 in Baltimore, was a leading African-American poet and writer. She was also an ardent activist in the abolitionist and women's rights movements.

After losing her mother at a young age, Harper was raised by an aunt. She attended a school for African-American children run by her uncle and then began working as a servant, where she had access to a library. In 1845, Harper published her first collection of poetry, titled *Forest Leaves*. In 1850 Frances began teaching domestic skills at a school run by leading abolitionist, John Brown. She became dedicated to the abolitionist cause.

In 1854, Harper published *Poems of Miscellaneous Subjects*, which featured one of her most famous works, 'Bury Me in a Free Land'. She also became a popular abolitionist lecturer, appearing with Frederick Douglass, William Garrison, Lucretia Mott and Lucy Stone. Harper made literary history in 1859 when she published *Two Offers*, becoming the first African-American female writer to publish a short story. The following year she married Fenton Harper and in 1862 she gave birth to a daughter, Mary Frances wrote several poems which explored her experiences during the reconstruction. She published her most famous novel *Lola Leroy* in 1892. Many women abolitionists wrote about slavery, but black women like Frances, brought their own direct experience to the subject.

In 1986, Frances was a cofounder of the National Association of Colored Women (NACW) with Ida Wells and Harriet Tubman. The organization campaigned for the rights of African-American women. Harper continued to support women's suffrage and the NACW. She died of heart failure on 22 February 1911, in Philadelphia, and was buried next to her daughter, Mary, at Eden Cemetery.

Bury me in a free land

Make me a grave where'er you will,
In a lowly plain, or a lofty hill;
Make it among earth's humblest graves,
But not in a land where men are slaves.

I could not rest if around my grave
I heard the steps of a trembling slave;
His shadow above my silent tomb
Would make it a place of fearful gloom.

I could not rest if I heard the tread
Of a coffle gang to the shambles led,
And the mother's shriek of wild despair
Rise like a curse on the trembling air.

I could not sleep if I saw the lash
Drinking her blood at each fearful gash,
And I saw her babes torn from her breast,
Like trembling doves from their parent nest.

I'd shudder and start if I heard the bay
Of bloodhounds seizing their human prey,
And I heard the captive plead in vain
As they bound afresh his galling chain.

If I saw young girls from their mother's arms
Bartered and sold for their youthful charms,
My eye would flash with a mournful flame,
My death-paled cheek grow red with shame.

I would sleep, dear friends, where bloated might
Can rob no man of his dearest right;
My rest shall be calm in any grave
Where none can call his brother a slave.

I ask no monument, proud and high,
To arrest the gaze of the passers by;
All that my yearning spirit craves,
Is bury me not in a land of slaves.

6 April
Writer, soldier and revolutionary: Larissa Reissner (1895-1926)

Larissa Reissner was born in Lublin, Poland. Between 1903 and 1907, her family was forced to live in exile in Berlin because her father's activism put the family at risk. After 1905 Russian Revolution, the family moved to Saint Petersburg Larissa attended St Petersburg University.

After the February Revolution, Larissa began to write for Maxim Gorky's paper *New Life*. She also took part in the Provisional Government's teaching programme, working with workers' and sailors' clubs in Petrograd.

After the Bolshevik Revolution, Reisner helped the newly appointed People's Commissar, Anatoly Lunacharsky, to win support for the revolution among artists and poets. Later, she worked at the Smolny Institute with Lunacharsky, cataloguing art treasures.

She became a member of the Bolshevik Party in 1918. During the Civil War, she was a soldier and a political commissar of the Red Army. She served as chief of an intelligence section of the Volga River flotilla in August 1918 battle for Sviazhsk. During 1919, she served as the Commissar at the Naval Staff Headquarters in Moscow. In 1921, she and her husband travelled to Afghanistan as representatives of the Soviet Republic.

In October 1923 Larissa travelled illegally to Germany to witness the revolution there first-hand and to write about it, producing collections of articles entitled *Berlin, October 1923* and *Hamburg at the Barricades*. During 1924-1925, she worked as a special correspondent for *Izvestiya*, (News) and she adopted a boy by the name of Alyosha Makarov. She also worked on Leon Trotsky's Commission for the Improvement of Industrial Products.

Larissa died on 9 February 1926, in the Kremlin Hospital, from typhoid; she was thirty years old.

7 April
Radical and gay: Eliza Cook (1818 - 1889)

Eliza Cook was a hugely popular English author, editor and poet associated with the Chartist movement. She was the youngest of the eleven children of a brass-worker living in London Road, Southwark and was entirely self-educated. A radical and Owenite socialist, Eliza was a proponent of political freedom for women, and her idea of 'levelling up' made her hugely popular with the working-class public in both England and America. Her *Eliza Cook's Journal* outsold Charles Dickens' Household Words and she wrote hugely popular poems in support of the Charter and other radical causes.

Eliza had a long sexual relationship with an American actress, Charlotte Cushman. The couple caused a stir by wearing matching outfits, often including

male clothes, and cutting their hair short. In later life, Eliza suffered from illhealth and survived on royalties. She moved in with her sister and died there in 1890.

In 'A song for the workers', Eliza challenged Victorian conventions by celebrating the nobility of the labour of women as well as men, and pointed to the physical, mental and emotional aspects of exploitation.

A Song for the Workers

Let Man toil to win his living,
    Work is not a task to spurn;
Poor is gold of others' giving,
    To the silver that we earn.
Let Man proudly take his station
    At the smithy, loom, or plough;
The richest crown-pearls in a nation
    Hang from Labour's reeking brow.

Though her hand grows hard with duty,
    Filling up the common Fate;
Let fair Woman's cheek of beauty
    Never blush to own its state.

Let fond Woman's heart of feeling
    Never be ashamed to spread
Industry and honest dealing,
    As a barter for her bread.

Work on bravely, GOD 's own daughters!
    Work on stanchly, GOD 's own sons!
But when Life has too rough waters,
    Truth must fire her minute guns.

Shall ye be unceasing drudges?
    Shall the cry upon your lips
Never make your selfish judges
 Less severe with Despot-whips?

Shall the mercy that we cherish,
    As old England's primest boast,
See no slaves but those who perish
    On a far and foreign coast?

When we reckon hives of money,
    Owned by Luxury and Ease,
Is it just to grasp the honey
    While Oppression chokes the bees?

Is it just the poor and lowly
    Should be held as soulless things?
Have they not a claim as holy
    As rich men, to angels' wings?

Shall we burthen Boyhood's muscle?
    Shall the young Girl mope and lean,
Till we hear the dead leaves rustle
    On a tree that should be green?

Shall we bar the brain from thinking
    Of aught else than work and woe?
Shall we keep parched lips from drinking
    Where refreshing waters flow?

Shall we strive to shut out Reason,
    Knowledge, Liberty, and Health?
Shall all Spirit-light be treason
    To the mighty King of Wealth?

Shall we stint with niggard measure,
    Human joy, and human rest?
Leave no profit—give no pleasure,
    To the toiler's human breast?

Shall our Men, fatigued to loathing.
    Plod on sickly, worn, and bowed?
Shall our Maidens sew fine clothing,
    Dreaming of their own, white shroud?

No! for Right is up and asking
    Loudly for a juster lot;
And Commerce must not let her tasking
    Form a nation's canker spot.

Work on bravely, GOD 's own daughters!
    Work on stanchly, GOD 's own sons!
But till ye have smoother waters,
    Let Truth fire her minute guns!

The March of the Weavers in Berlin: Käthe Kollwitz 1897

8 April
The Art of Resistance: Käthe Kollwitz (1867-1945)

Käthe Kollwitz's artistic work depicts war and revolution and champions the dispossessed. Käthe Schmid was born in Kaliningrad, daughter of a bricklayer. Barred from studying art in her hometown because she was a woman, she moved to Berlin and Munich to pursue her education. There, she met radical artists and married socialist Karl Kollwitz, a medical doctor. Kollwitz's breakthrough work was the cycle 'The Weavers', which focuses on resistance against social injustice. Kollwitz's second cycle, 'The Peasant War', invoked the German uprising of the 1520s, and also centres on the rebellion of the exploited against social injustice. 'The Peasant War' series includes some of Kollwitz's greatest achievements: 'Ploughing', 'Raped', 'Sharpening the Scythe', 'Arming in the Vault', 'Outbreak' and 'The Prisoners', which explored different aspects of working-class oppression and resistance. 'After the Battle' depicts a mother's nighttime search for

Käthe Kollwitz. *Aufruhr* (Uprising), 1899

her son among the dead left on a battlefield. Loss and grieving became a central theme in Kollwitz's work after the death of her son, Peter, in the early days of the World War I. She conveys a profound sense of tragedy and of human responsibility to fight against death-spawning militarism and war.

In 1919, Käthe Kollwitz began work on the woodcut cycle. In 'The Volunteers' Kollwitz depicts her son Peter beside Death, who leads a group of young men to war in a frenzied procession. Kollwitz created a universal condemnation of such slaughter.

In January 1919, at the height of the German Revolution, right-wing militias assassinated the revolutionary leader Karl Liebknecht. Kathe responded with her famous woodcut 'In Memoriam: Karl Liebknecht', a moving tribute to this communist leader. In 1924, Kollwitz created her three most famous posters: 'Germany's Children Starving', 'Bread', and 'Never Again War'. After the Nazi rise to power, in the mid 1930s, Kollwitz completed her last great cycle of eight lithographs, Death. Death was never far from Kathe. Her husband Karl died of illness in 1940 and two years later her grandson Peter fell victim to Hitler's war.

Käthe Kollwitz. *Never Again War* 1924

Käthe Kollwitz died on 22 April, 1945, just a few days before World War II ended. Kollwitz's images are profound indictments of the violence, injustice and inhumanity of capitalism.

9 April
Republicanism, suffrage and socialism: Constance Gore Boothe, later Countess Markievicz (1868-1927)
Eva Gore Roper (1870-1926)

Sisters Constance and Eva Gore Booth were born in London to a family of wealthy Irish Protestants. In 1896 Eva met Esther Roper while travelling in Italy and they established a life-long relationship, living together first in Manchester and then in London. Constance was presented at court to Queen Victoria in 1887 and later married a Polish Count, Casimir Markievicz. In 1903 Eva and Esther established the Lancashire and Cheshire Women's Textile and Other Workers Representation Committee. That year they also they organized a women's suffrage petition which attracted over 30,000 signatures from the textile districts. Eva coedited *Women's Labour News*, which campaigned to unite women workers. She was active in the Independent Labour Party. In 1908 Eva and Constance campaigned together against Liberal Party candidate Winston Churchill in the parliamentary election in Manchester North West.

Eva and Constance

In 1909 Constance was living in Ireland, where she became known to British intelligence for her role in the Irish nationalist movement and a militant women's organisation. She worked closely with the militant labour leaders, James Larkin and James Connolly. During the 1913 Dublin Lockout she worked tirelessly to provide food for the workers' families.

In 1914 Eva and Esther opposed World War I and helped establish the Women's Peace Crusade. Other members included Charlotte Despard and

Selina Cooper. Meanwhile Constance helped organise and train the Irish Citizen Army. In May 1916 she took part in the Easter Rising and became the only woman to be courtmartialled. In court she declared: 'I did what I thought was right, and I stand by it'. The court reached a unique verdict: 'Guilty. Death by being shot', but with a recommendation to mercy 'solely and only on account of her sex'. The sentence was commuted to penal servitude for life. Eva was the leading figure who organised the successful reprieve of the death sentence passed on her sister.

Constance served thirteen months in gaol and in the General Election, December 1918, she became the first woman ever returned to the Commons at Westminster, but as a member for Sinn Féin she did not take her seat. Instead she served as

Minister of Labour (April 1919-21) in the first Dail.

Eva Gore-Booth died of cancer in Hampstead on 30th June 1926 with Esther Roper at her side. Constance died in a Dublin hospital in 1927 and the working-class people of the city lined the streets for her funeral.

Countess Markievicz

Poem:
Bobby Sands: The Rhythm of Time

Bobby Sands was the leader of the 1981 hunger strike in which Irish republican prisoners protested against the removal of Special Category Status. During his strike, he was elected to the British Parliament as an Anti H-Block candidate in a huge act of defiance against British rule. Bobby, and nine other prisoners, died while on hunger strike. He was twenty-seven years old. Bobby was also a poet.

There's an inner thing in every man,
Do you know this thing my friend?
It has withstood the blows of a million years,
And will do so to the end.

It was born when time did not exist,
And it grew up out of life,
It cut down evil's strangling vines,
Like a slashing searing knife.

It lit fires when fires were not,
And burnt the mind of man,
Tempering leadened hearts to steel,
From the time that time began.

It wept by the waters of Babylon,
And when all men were a loss,
It screeched in writhing agony,
And it hung bleeding from the Cross.

It died in Rome by lion and sword,
And in defiant cruel array,
When the deathly word was 'Spartacus'
Along the Appian Way.

It marched with Wat the Tyler's poor,
And frightened lord and king,
And it was emblazoned in their deathly stare,
As e'er a living thing.

It smiled in holy innocence,
Before conquistadors of old,
So meek and tame and unaware,
Of the deathly power of gold.

It burst forth through pitiful Paris streets,
And stormed the old Bastille,
And marched upon the serpent's head,
And crushed it 'neath its heel.

It died in blood on Buffalo Plains,
And starved by moons of rain,
Its heart was buried in Wounded Knee,
But it will come to rise again.

It screamed aloud by Kerry lakes,
As it was knelt upon the ground,
And it died in great defiance,
As they coldly shot it down.

It is found in every light of hope,
It knows no bounds nor space
It has risen in red and black and white,
It is there in every race.

It lies in the hearts of heroes dead,
It screams in tyrants' eyes,
It has reached the peak of mountains high,
It comes searing 'cross the skies.

It lights the dark of this prison cell,
It thunders forth its might,
It is 'the undauntable thought', my friend,
That thought that says 'I'm right!'

10 April
Red Democrat, poet & novellist: Louise Otto Peters (1815-1895)

Louise Otto Peters was born in 1819 to a middle-class family and educated at home by a radical father. After his death, she established herself as a writer to support herself and her sisters, publishing socially committed novels and poems. Her 1845 book, *Schloss und Fabrik* (Castle and Factory), was influenced by Frederick Engels' *Condition of the British Working Classes* and explored the possibility of women's freedom. The work was censored by the German government because it exposed treatment of both male and female factory workers. It was not published in full until the censored version was made public in 1989.

Louise moved to Leipzig in 1848, where she participated in the revolution and became known as 'The Red Democrat'. In 1849 she founded the '*Frauen-Zeitung*' (Woman Worker), a newspaper devoted to women's issues, which carried the motto: 'Female Citizens in the Republic of Liberty'. Otto was so famous that when the government of Saxony introduced a law to stop women editing newspapers, it became known as the 'Otto Law'.

In 1858 Louise married the writer and journalist August Peters. The couple had fallen in love during the 1848 revolution, but August served seven years in prison because of his activism. In October 1865, Louise helped to establish the General German Women's Association, which campaigned for economic and political rights for women.

The next German women to edit a paper was Clara Zetkin in 1891. Zetkin paid this tribute to Otto-Peters: 'She wanted to put into practice the dream she had in the 1849s: full equality for her sex; full equality for workers'.

The Lace-Makers (1840)

See the women making lace
Pallid cheeks and eyes so red!
Tired out, and all for nothing,
Nothing but the coarsest bread!

Grandma's eyes are blinded now,
Only death will set her free,
Wringing hands, she quietly prays:
God help us in extremity.

The children move their little hands,
Up and down the bobbins fling.
Toil and trouble without end
Is what their future life will bring.

God protect each little Miss
Who nothing knows of youthful zest –
For poverty embraces all;
Want snuggles into every breast.
See the women making lace,
Pillow lace, a work of art;
Rich and famous – do not scruples
Linger in your inner heart?

Frauen-Zeitung'
(Woman Worker)

While they decline, you feast and spend,
And savour life in luxury,
Meanwhile these women starve and die,
Released, at last from misery!

See the women making lace
Is not your faith hypocrisy?
All their belief extinguished now,
They call your faith apostasy!

See the woman making lace,
Have you no mercy for her plight?
For else your final waking hour
Will reap her curse from pain and blight!

Poem:
Siegfried Sassoon: The General, 1917

'Good-morning, good-morning!' the General said
When we met him last week on our way to the line.
Now the soldiers he smiled at are most of 'em dead,
And we're cursing his staff for incompetent swine.
'He's a cheery old card,' grunted Harry to Jack
As they slogged up to Arras with rifle and pack.

But he did for them both by his plan of attack.

Photograph: IWM

11 April
Revolutionary Socialist: Clara Zetkin (1857-1933)

Clara Eissner, the daughter of a schoolteacher was born in Saxony in 1857. When the Social Democratic Party (SDP) was formed in 1875, Clara joined up. In 1878 Otto von Bismarck introduced the anti-socialist law which banned SDP meetings and publications so Clara left Germany to live in exile in Zurich and then Paris. Clara married Ossip Zetkin, a Russian revolutionary who was also living in exile. Ossip was a carpenter and a Marxist. In 1883, her son Maxim, was born, followed by Kostya in 1885.

Ossip Zetkin died of tuberculosis in January 1889. Clara continued with her political campaigns, focusing on supporting women workers. When Bismark's anti-socialist laws were lifted in 1890, Zetkin returned to Germany. Membership of the SDP grew rapidly. In 1891 Clara Zetkin became editor of the SPD's journal, *Die Gleichheit* (Equality). Zetkin changed her views on women's suffrage, which she had dismissed as a middle-class movement, and helped to organize the first International Conference of Socialist Women. Clara initiated International Women's Day in 1910 at an International Conference of Working Women in Copenhagen.

Clara campaigned with Rosa Luxemburg and Karl Liebknecht against the right wing of the party. This fight came to a head when war broke out on 4 August, 1914. While the leaders of the socialist parties across Europe collapsed into nationalism, Zetkin, Luxemburg and Liebknecht were among a group of socialists who opposed the war. Clara used her position as editor of *Die Gleichheit* and as Secretary of the Women's Secretariat of the Socialist International to campaign for the anti-war movement at international conferences.

The left began to organise growing anger against the war. They set up the Spartacus League which

initiated demonstrations, arguing that socialists should turn nationalist conflict into revolutionary war. On 28th June 1916, Liebknecht was arrested and 55,000 munitions workers went on strike.

In April 1917 Clara Zetkin joined other left-wing members of the SDP and formed the Independent Social Democratic Party (USPD).

The German Revolution began with a naval mutiny on 4 November 1918. Within hours, the naval town of Kiel was firmly in the hands of about 40,000 rebellious sailors, soldiers and workers. By 8 November, workers councils had sprang up in every major town and city in Germany.

The leaders of the SDP were now in government and rushed to deflect the revolution. They set up a provisional government and announced elections to a constitutional assembly would be held. On 5 January, the leader of the parliamentary socialists, Fredrick Ebert, called in the German Army and the Freikorps to bring an end to the uprising in Berlin. By January 1919 the rebellion had been crushed. Rosa Luxemburg and Karl Liebknecht, who refused to flee the city, were captured on 16 January, taken to the Freikorps headquarters and murdered. Clara was devastated by the death of her great friends and comrades but continued to fight. In January 1919, she was the first women to speak in the German parliament. Her speech was an attack on Friedrich Ebert.

In January 1919, the Spartacus League changed its name to the German Communist Party (KPD). Clara served on the Central Committee of the KPD. She was also appointed to the exec-utive committee of Comintern. A life-long anti-racist, Zetkin took part in the international pro-tests against Jim Crow laws in the United States and campaigned against the racist conviction of the Scotsboro Boys.

In 1932, Zetkin, although 75 years old, was once again elected to the Reichstag. In her speech, she denounced the Nazi Party. Clara Zetkin died on 20 June, 1933.

12 April
Abolitionist and Suffragist: Sarah Parker Remond (1826-1894)

Sarah was born in 1826 in Salem, Massachusetts, one of eight siblings. Her older brother, Charles Lenox Redmond, became an anti-slavery lecturer and sisters Nancy, Caroline, and Sarah, were active in the Salem Female Anti-Slavery Society, founded by a group of black women, which included Sarah's mother, in 1832. The Redmond children suffered from racism and Sarah was refused admission to Salem's high school. The family had to move to Rhode Island so the daughters could attend a private school for African-American children.

In 1842, when Sarah was sixteen, she gave her first public lecture on the horrors of slavery. Many more were to follow. In 1853 Sarah attended an opera and refused to leave a section reserved for whites. When a policeman forcibly ejected her, she fell down some stairs. She sued in a civil suit, winning five hundred dollars and an end to segregated seating at the hall.

In 1856, Sarah toured New York lecturing on behalf of the American Anti-Slavery Society. She shocked audiences by describing the sexual violence endured by female slaves. In 1859 she sailed to Liverpool to begin a lecture tour of Britain. Sarah wrote to a friend, 'I fear not the wind and the waves, I know however I go, the spirit of prejudice will greet me'. At her overflowing UK lectures, Redmond told audiences of thousands of the evils of slavery and of the discrimination and indignities suffered by free black people in the US. She was thought to be the first woman to denounce slavery in front of mass audiences. Thousands of working men and women in the textile districts of Lancashire heard Sarahs' powerful denunciations of slavery: 'I appeal on behalf of four million men, women and children who are chattels in the Southern States of America, not because they are identical with my race and colour, though I am proud of that identity, but because they are men and women'.

During the American Civil War, the campaign led by Sarah and other black activists played a role in cementing support for the North among textile workers, despite the hardships caused by the blockade of US cotton. Karl Marx wrote that this support for the north was one of the highest points reached by the British working class.

Sarah became the first black woman to enrol at Bedford College in London, a college offering education to women. She also became a founder member of the influential Ladies' London Emancipation Society. After the war, she raised funds to support free black people and campaigned against British brutality against slave rebellions.

Sarah moved to Florence, Italy. She enrolled at a medical college and fulfilled a lifelong ambition by training as a nurse. She married an Italian man in 1877. Sarah died in Rome in 1894 and was buried there in the Protestant cemetery.

In a speech she delivered in Liverpool in 1859, Sarah stated:

■ I appeal on behalf of four millions of men, women, and children who are chattels in the Southern States of America, not because they are identical with my race and color, though I am proud of that identity, but because they are men and women. The sum of sixteen hundred millions of dollars is invested in their bones, sinews, and flesh — is this not sufficient reason why all the friends of humanity should not endeavor with all their might and power, to overturn the vile systems of slavery.

Poem
Amelia Opie: The Black Man's Lament (1826)

A melia Opie was a radical Quaker and supporter of the London
Corresponding Society. She wrote The 'Black Man's Lament, or
How to make Sugar' as her contribution against slavery.

Come, listen to my plaintive ditty,
Ye tender hearts, and children dear!
And, should it move souls to pity,
Oh! try to end the griefs you

There is a beauteous plant, that grows
In western India's sultry clime,
Which makes, alas! the Black man's woes,
And also makes the White man's crime.

For know, its tall gold stems contain
A sweet rich juice, which White men prize;
And that they may this sugar gain,
The Negro toils, and bleeds, and dies.

But, Negro slave! thyself shall tell,
Of past and present wrongs the story;
And would all British hearts could feel,
To end those wrongs were Britain's glory.

Negro speaks:

First to our own dear Negro land,
His ships the cruel White man sends;
And there contrives, by armed band,
o tear us from our homes and friends;

From parents, brethren's fond embrace;
From tender wife, and child to tear;
Then in a darksome ship to place,
Pack'd close, like bales of cotton there.

Oh! happy those, who, in that hour,
Die from their prison's putrid breath!
Since they escape from White man's pow'r,
From toils and stripes, and lingering death!

For what awaited us on shore,
Soon as the ship had reach'd the strand,
Unloading its degraded store
Of freemen, forc'd from Negro land.

See! eager White men come around,

To choose and claim us for their slaves;
And make us envy those who found
In the dark ship their early graves.

They bid black men and women stand
In lines, the drivers in the rear:
Poor Negroes hold a hoe in hand,
But they the wicked cart-whip bear.

Then we, in gangs, like beasts in droves,
Swift to the cane-fields driven are;
There first our toil the weeds removes,
And next we holes for plants

But woe to all, both old and young,
Women and men, or strong or weak,
Worn out or fresh, those gangs among,
That dare the toilsome line to break!

As holes must all at once be made,
Together we must work or stop;
Therefore, the whip our strength must aid,
And lash us when we pause or drop!

When we have dug sufficient space,
The bright-eye top of many a cane,
Lengthways, we in the trenches place,
And then we trenches dig again.

We cover next the plants with mould;
And e'en, ere fifteen days come round,
We can the slender sprouts behold,
Just shooting greenly from the ground.

The weeds about them clear'd away,
Then mould again by hand we throw;
And, at no very distant day,
Here Negroes plough, and there they hoe.

But when the crops are ripen'd quite,
Tis then begin our saddest pains;
For then we toil both day and night,
Though fever burns within our veins.

13 April
The Indefatigable Anne Knight (1786–1862)

Anne was born in Chelmsford in 1781 to a family of Quakers who were social reformers. In the 1830s Anne set up a women's anti-slavery society in Chelmsford. In 1833 she initiated a national women's petition against slavery. It was signed by 298,785 women, the largest anti-slavery petition in the movement's history.

In 1834 Anne toured France where she gave lectures on need for the immediate abolition of slavery without compensation. She attended the World Anti-Slavery Convention held at Exeter Hall in London, in June 1840 but as a woman was refused permission to speak. This experience propelled Anne to connect the campaign for the abolition of slavery with that for women's rights.

In 1847 Anne published a leaflet which argued, 'Never will the nations of the earth be well governed, until both sexes, as well as all parties, are fully represented and have a hand in the enactment and administration of the laws'. Knight became active in the Chartist movement despite criticising them for not supporting women's right to vote. In a letter published in the *Brighton Herald* in 1850 she demanded that the Chartists should campaign for what she described as 'true universal suffrage'.

In 1848 Anne was in Paris. She was active in the revolution, joining with French female socialists lead by Jeanne Deroin to press for women's rights. In 1851 Anne Knight and Anne Kent established the Sheffield Female Political Association. Anne developed her own campaigning techniques, which included writing slogans on the envelopes of letters she sent and wearing ribbons with slogans. Later that year the Association published an 'Address to the Women of England', which was presented to parliament. This was the first mass petition that demanded women's suffrage.

Anne Knight died on 4 November, 1862.

14 April
The insurgent Communard: Elisabeth Dmitrieff (1850-?)

E lisabeth was born in Russia, the daughter of a Tsarist official but rebelled against her background. She was active in her youth in the Socialist circles of Saint Petersburg. In 1868, she travelled to Switzerland, and co-founded the Russian section of the First International. Delegat-ed to London, she met Karl Marx and spent months with the Marx family becoming friends with Laura, Jenny and Eleanor. In March 1871, when Elisabeth was only twenty-one, Marx delegated her to cover the events of the Commune. She became one its greatest women leaders.

Working with Nathalie Lemel, Elisabeth helped to set up the Women's Union for the Defense of Paris and Care of the Wounded and co-founded the Women's Union. She campaigned for women's education and the right to vote, raising women's concerns and organising cooperative workshops. Elisabeth also contributed to the socialist newspaper *La Cause du peuple* (The Cause of the People). After having fought on the barricades during the final 'Bloody Week' of the Commune, Elisabeth fled to Russia. Once arrived in her native country, she married a man who was later convicted of fraud and in 1878 followed him in deportation to Siberia, where she disappeared from public view.

15 April
'Ain't I a Woman?' Sojourner Truth (1797-1883)

Sojourner Truth was born a slave named Isabella Boumfree in New York in 1797. She was bought and sold four times and subjected to harsh physical labour and violent punishments. In her teens, she was united with another slave with whom she had five children. In late 1826 Truth ran away with her infant Sophia to a nearby abolitionist family. The family bought her freedom for twenty dollars and helped her successfully sue for the return of her son Peter, who had been illegally sold into slavery in Alabama. Sojourner was the first black woman to sue a white man. Sojourner moved to New York City in 1828, where she worked for a local minister. In 1843, she declared that the Spirit called on her to preach the truth and renamed herself Sojourner Truth. She met leading radical abolitionists including William Lloyd Garrison and Frederick Douglass. Sojourner never learned to read or write and in 1850, she dictated what would become her autobiography— *The Narrative of Sojourner Truth*. She survived on sales of the book.

In 1851, Sojourner began a lecture tour that included a women's rights conference in Akron, Ohio, where she delivered her famous 'Ain't I a Woman?' speech which challenged the racism of the women's rights movement and asserted the rights of black women.

During the 1850's, Sojourner settled in Michigan. She continued speaking nationally and helped slaves escape to freedom. When the Civil War started, she organized supplies for black troops. After the war, she helped freed slaves find jobs and build new lives. While in Washington DC, she lobbied against segregation and in the mid 1860s, when a streetcar conductor tried to violently block her from riding, she ensured he was arrested and prosecuted. In the late 1860s, she collected thousands of signatures on a petition to provide former slaves with land, though Congress never took action. Nearly blind and deaf towards the end of her life, Sojourner spent her final years in Michigan.

Sojourner's speech:
'That man over there says that women need to be helped into carriages, and lifted over ditches, and to have the best place everywhere. Nobody ever helps me into carriages, or over mud-puddles, or gives me any best place! And ai'n't I a woman? Look at me! Look at my arm! I have ploughed and planted, and gathered into barns, and no man could head me! And ai'n't I a woman?
I could work as much and eat as much as a man - when I could get it - and bear the lash as well! And ain't I a woman?
I have borne thirteen children, and seen most all sold off to slavery, and when I cried out with my mother's grief, none but Jesus heard me! And ain't I a woman?
Then they talk about this thing in the head; what's this they call it? [member of audience whispers, "intellect"] That's it, honey. What's that got to do with women's rights or negroes' rights? If my cup won't hold but a pint, and yours holds a quart, wouldn't you be mean not to let me have my little half measure full?
Then that little man in black there, he says women can't have as much rights as men, 'cause Christ wasn't a woman! Where did your Christ come from? Where did your Christ come from? From God and a woman! Man had nothing to do with Him.
If the first woman God ever made was strong enough to turn the world upside down all alone, these women together ought to be able to turn it back and get it right side up again!
And now they is asking to do it, the men better let them. Obliged to you for hearing me, and now old Sojourner ain't got nothing more to say.'

16 April
Suffragist, pacifist, communist: Dora Montefiore (1851-1933)

Dora Fuller was born on 20 December, 1851. She was educated at home, and then at a private school in Brighton. In 1874 she went to Australia, where she met George Barrow Mon-tefiore, a wealthy businessman. They lived in Sydney, where their daughter was born in 1883 and their son in 1887, but her husband died on 17 July, 1889. She became an advocate of women's rights and in March 1891 she established the Womanhood Suffrage League of New South Wales.

On returning to England in 1892, Dora worked with Millicent Fawcett at the National Union of Suffrage Societies. She also joined the socialist Social Democratic Federation and eventually served on its executive and wrote for its journal, *Justice*.

During the Boer War, Dora refused to pay income tax because 'such tax went towards financing a war in the making of which I had had no voice'. Bailiffs sold her goods at public auctions. Dora joined the Women's Social and Political Union (WSPU) in 1905 and worked closely with Sylvia Pank-hurst in London. In 1906 Dora refused to pay taxes until women won the vote. She hung a banner outside her house with the slogan, 'Women should vote for the laws they obey and the taxes they pay' and she was besieged by bailiffs for six weeks.

In October 1906 Dora was arrested during a WSPU demonstration and was sent to Holloway prison. Soon after, she left the WSPU but remained close to Sylvia Pankhurst. In the autumn of 1907 Dora and seventy other women left the WSPU to form the more democratic Women's Freedom League (WFL). In 1907 Montefiore joined the more socialist-leaning

Adult Suffrage Society and was elected its honorary secretary. She also remained in the Social Democratic Federation and was a delegate to the International Socialist Congress of 1907 (other delegates in-cluded Vladimir Lenin, Rosa Luxemburg and Clara Zetkin). Dora was an increasingly vocal critic of militarism and a leading activist in support of workers during the Dublin Lockout of 1913. She joined the British Socialist Party and played a part in the discussions which led to the establishment of the British Communist Party in July 1920. She was elected to its Executive Committee.
In 1921, Dora's son died from the delayed effects of a mustard gas attack on the western front. She returned to Australia and became active in the Australian Communist Party. In bad health she returned to Britain and died on 21 December, 1933, at her home in Hastings.

There is a letter from Alexandra Kollontai to Dora Mon-tefiore at: *https://www.marxists.org/ archive/kollonta/1920/letter-from-russia.htm*

Dora speaking outside her house

Poem:
Walt Whitman: The Wound Dresser

Walt Whitman was America's greatest poet, a radical and a democrat. During the American Civil War he volunteered as a nurse. In this poem, he recounts his memories.

The Wound Dresser

On, on I go, (open doors of time! open hospital doors!)
The crush'd head I dress, (poor crazed hand tear not the bandage away,)
The neck of the cavalry-man with the bullet through and through I examine,
Hard the breathing rattles, quite glazed already the eye, yet life struggles hard,
(Come sweet death! be persuaded O beautiful death!
In mercy come quickly.)

From the stump of the arm, the amputated hand,
I undo the clotted lint, remove the slough, wash off the matter and blood,
Back on his pillow the soldier bends with curv'd neck and side falling head,
His eyes are closed, his face is pale, he dares not look on the bloody stump,
And has not yet look'd on it.

I dress a wound in the side, deep, deep,
But a day or two more, for see the frame all wasted and sinking,
And the yellow-blue countenance see.

I dress the perforated shoulder, the foot with the bullet-wound,
Cleanse the one with a gnawing and putrid gangrene, so sickening, so offensive,
While the attendant stands behind aside me holding the tray and pail.

I am faithful, I do not give out,
The fractur'd thigh, the knee, the wound in the abdomen,
These and more I dress with impassive hand, (yet deep in my breast a fire, a burning flame.)

4
Thus in silence in dreams' projections,
Returning, resuming, I thread my way through the hospitals,
The hurt and wounded I pacify with soothing hand,
I sit by the restless all the dark night, some are so young,
Some suffer so much, I recall the experience sweet and sad,
(Many a soldier's loving arms about this neck have cross'd and rested,
Many a soldier's kiss dwells on these bearded lips.)

17 April
Fighting for the right to care: Mary Mahoney (1845-1926)

M ary Mahoney was the first black American woman to complete nurse's training in 1879. Mary was born on 7 May, 1845, in Boston, Massachusetts. She challenged racist discrimination to be ad-mitted to the nursing school of the New England Hospital for Women and Children and became the first black woman to complete nurse's training in 1879.

Mahoney campaigned against the racism which was deeply rooted in the American nursing pro-fession. In 1896, she joined the Nurses Associated Alumnae of the United States and Canada (NAAUSC). The NAAUSC consisted mainly of white members, many holding openly racist views. Mahoney believed that a group was needed to advocate for the equality of African-American nurses. In 1908, she co-founded the National Association of Colored Graduate Nurses (NA-CGN). In the following year, at the NACGN's first national convention, Mary gave the opening speech. At the convention, the organization's members elected Mahoney to be the national chaplain and gave her a life membership.

Mary was one of the first women to register to vote in Boston fol-lowing the ratification of the 19th Amendment in 1920. She was inducted into both the Nursing Hall of Fame and the Na-tional Women's Hall of Fame. She died in Boston in 1926.

18 April
Factory girl, socialist and writer: Ethel Carnie Holdsworth
(1886-1962)

Ethel Carnie was born into a weaving family in Oswaldtwistle, Lancashire. She started working part-time in a mill at age eleven and worked full-time from the age of thirteen. In her later articles for the *Woman Worker*, she described her earlier experiences as 'slavery'.

Ethel attended Great Harwood British School from 1892 until 1899. She was a passionate read-er, often snatching moments to read while operating machinery at work. Her first book of poems, R*hymes from the Factory,* was published in 1907, when Ethel was just twenty-one years old. When the volume was republished in 1908, she won national recognition. The socialist Robert Blatchford, owner of *The Clarion* newspaper, offered Ethel a job writing for the *Woman Worker*, in London. She edited the paper between July and December 1909.

A second book of poems, *Songs of a Factory Girl*, was published in 1911, and her third and final collection of poems, *Voices of Womanhood*, followed three years later. Her themes relate to the things she had seen in life: the slavery of the factory system and of domestic service, women exhausted by work as well as family and domestic life. But what speaks most strongly is Ethel's determination to stand up for the women of her class and win support for the fight for socialism.

Ethel Carnie was a member of the Co-operative Society and the Independent Labour Party. She protested against the introduction of conscription in World War I and addressed 20,000 women during the Women's Peace Crusade. During the 1920s she lived in Hebden Bridge with her husband Alfred Holdsworth, who she had married in 1915. Ethel opposed the rise of Stalin and edited a newspaper, *The Clear Light*, which campaigned for the left to unite against capitalism, militarism and religion.

In 1924, *The Clear Light* threw its support behind
the National Union for Combatting Fascism while
continuing to highlight how members of the British
royal family and upper classes were supporting
fascism.

Ethel was the first working-class woman to publish
best-selling novels. *Helen of Four Gates* was made
into a film in 1924. The novel *This Slavery* (1925)
is about a strike and the characters are working-class socialists who read Marx's *Capital*. The
book is dedicated 'To Mother and Father, slaves
and rebels [...] with a Daughter's affection and a
Comrade's greetings'. This is from Rachel's speech:
'I wonder when women'll be free, mother An'
chaps, too, of course. But we, we somehow have a
tradition behind us besides an economic slavery.
We've got the race on our shoulders, an' all th'
other besides'.

'Our Right to Play', the *Woman Worker*, 14 April,
1909

'For God's sake, women, go out and play.
'Instead of staring round to see what wants polish-
ing or rubbing, go out into the open and draw the
breath of the moors or the hills into your lungs. Get
some of the starshine and sunlight into your souls,
and do not forget that you are something more
than a dish washer – that you are more necessary
to the human race than politicians – or anything.
Remember you belong to the aristocracy of labour
– the long pedigree of toil, and the birth-right
which Nature gives to everyone had entitled you to
an estate higher than that of princes'.

Poem:
Ella Wheeler Wilcox: Protest (1914)

Ella Wheeler Wilcox (1850-1919) was an American author and poet. Her works include *Poems of Passion and Solitude*, which contains the lines 'Laugh, and the world laughs with you; weep, and you weep alone'. Her autobiography, *The Worlds and I*, was published in 1918, a year before her death.

Protest

'To sin by silence, when we should protest,
Makes cowards out of men. The human race
Has climbed on protest. Had no voice been raised
Against injustice, ignorance, and lust,
The inquisition yet would serve the law,
And guillotines decide our least disputes.
The few who dare, must speak and speak again
To right the wrongs of many. Speech, thank God,
No vested power in this great day and land
Can gag or throttle. Press and voice may cry
Loud disapproval of existing ills;
May criticise oppression and condemn
The lawlessness of wealth-protecting laws
That let the children and childbearers toil
To purchase ease for idle millionaires.

Therefore I do protest against the boast
Of independence in this mighty land.

Call no chain strong, which holds one rusted link.
Call no land free, that holds one fettered slave.
Until the manacled slim wrists of babes
Are loosed to toss in childish sport and glee,
Until the mother bears no burden, save
The precious one beneath her heart, until
God's soil is rescued from the clutch of greed
And given back to labor, let no man
Call this the land of freedom'.

19 April
**Revolutionary socialist champion of worker's safety:
Crystal Eastman** (1881-1928)

'When the dead bodies of girls are found piled up against locked doors leading to exits after a factory fire, who wants to hear about a great relief fund? What we want is to start a revolution'. 'Three Essentials for Accident Prevention', July 1912.

Crystal Eastman was born in Massachusetts in 1881, but the family moved to Canadaigua, New York. Crystal lived with younger brother, Max, who shared her socialist activism in Greenwich Village. She got a degree in law in 1903 and used her expertise to campaign for worker's safety. Crystal's study, *Work Accidents and the Law* resulted in the first workers' compensation law, which she drafted in 1910. She explained her interest in industrial statistics: 'It seems a tame thing to drop suddenly from talk of revolution to talk of statistics, but I believe in statistics as much as I believe in revolution. And what is more, I believe statistics are good stuff to start a revolution with'.

In 1912 Max and Crystal worked on *The Masses*, a revolutionary magazine owned cooperatively by its editors, who included John Reed, Louise Bryant and novelist Upton Sinclair. The follow-

Crystal alongside memebrs of the Womens Peace Party

ing year, she helped to launch the Congressional Union of Women Suffrage. During World War I, she organised against American militarism and imperialism. In 1917, Crystal recalled that her Women's Peace Party greeted the outbreak of the Russian Revolution with, 'mad, glad joy'.

In 1919 *The Masses* was closed down by the authorities. Max and Crystal then co-founded another socialist magazine, *The Liberator*. Crystal made the dangerous journey to Hungary to give a first-hand account of the revolution, writing a series called, 'Inside Communist Hungary'. Crystal also helped to form the American Civil Liberties Union and became co-author of the Equal Rights Amendment. In the same year, Crystal organised a Feminist Congress. When she was black-listed in the red scare of 1919-20 she found work on radical journals, *Equal Rights* and *Time and Tide*. In the first issue of *The Liberator,* Crystal wrote, 'Never in all history before could one so joyfully and confidently enter upon the enterprise of publishing and propagating ideas. Dedicating our admiration to the fearless faith in scientific intelligence of Karl Marx, and our energy to hopes that are even beyond his, we issue THE LIBERATOR into a world whose possibilities of freedom and life for all, are now certainly immeasurable'. Crystal Eastman died in 1928 aged just 46.

20 April
Painting the revolution: Nadezhda Udaltsova (1885-1961)

Nadezhda was one of a group of Russian avant-guard painters who were part of a great flowering of creative experimentation following the Revolution of 1917.

Before the outbreak of war in 1914, Nadezhda studied painting in Paris, experimented with Con-structivism and later joined the Suprematist movement. In 1916, she joined Kazimir Malevich's Su-prematist group. Like many of her avant-garde contemporaries, Nadezhda embraced the Russian Revolution of October 1917. The artists developed new styles of art to express the energy and op-timism unleashed by the overthrow of the old regime. Nadezhda was elected to the Young Leftist Federation of the Professional Union of Artists and Painters and began work in various state cultural institutions, including the Moscow Proletkult.

In 1918, she joined the Free State Studios, first working as Malevich's assistant, and then heading up her own studio. She also collaborated with Aleksandr Rodchenko, Malevich and others on a newspaper entitled *Anarkhiia* (Anarchy).

In 1919, Nadezhda contributed eleven paintings to the Fifth State Exhibition. She married her second husband, the painter Alexander Drevin. When Vkhutemas, the Russian state art and technical school, was established in 1920, she was appointed professor and senior lecturer. In 1920 she also became a member of the Institute for Artistic Culture (InKhuK). InKhuK was set up to decide how art should develop and promote the new world they believed was being built in Russia.

This optimism and creativity were crushed by the rise of Stalin. In 1938 Nadezhda's husband was arrested then murdered by Stalin and Nadezhda was intimidated into silence until after Stalin's death 1953.

21 April
Chartist rabble-rouser: Susanna Inge (1820-1902)

Susanna Inge was born in Folkstone but at some point after her birth the family moved to London. Her father was a plumber and painter. Susanna had little schooling and only learnt to write at the age of sixteen. At the age of twenty-two she became one of a handful of women who braved ridicule and scorn to take to the public stage in support of the Charter, a mass working-class campaign for democracy.

In July 1842 Susanna burst into public attention with an address 'To the women of England' which appeared in the Chartist *Northern Star*. Susanna argued that women should, 'assist those men who will, nay, who do, place women in on equality with themselves in gaining their rights, and yours will be gained also'. Many bitterly opposed Susanna's defence of women's rights, sneering at her as a 'hen-Chartist' and some of those critics were on her own side.

In October 1842, a meeting was called at the Chartist Hall at 55 Old Bailey to set up a Female Chartist Association. A certain Mr Cohen declared he 'did not consider that nature intended women to partake of political rights'. To the audience's delight, Susanna bested Mr Cohen, arguing that, 'woman ought to be better educated, and that, if she were, so far as mental capacity, she would in every respect be the equal of men'.

After the Chartist Movement declined, Susanna Inge tried to make a living by writing. On 18 February, 1847, Susanna, who was not married, gave birth to a son, James McGregor. In 1857 Susanna MacGregor and her son emigrated to New York, settling in Brooklyn, where she found work as a fur sewer. She died on 26 December, 1902 at the age of 82.

22 April
Rent striker, suffragist and communist: Helen Crawfurd
(1877-1954)

Helen Jack was born in the Gorbals, a working-class area of Glasgow. Her mother worked a steam-loom and her father was a baker. Helen became active in the women's suffrage movement around 1900, and in 1910 she joined the radical Women's Social and Political Union (WSPU). In 1912, she smashed the windows of Jack Pease, Minister for Education, and received a one-month prison sentence. In March 1914, Helen was arrested at a public meeting and received another month in prison. She went on an eight-day hunger strike. She left the WSPU in protest at their support for World War I, and in 1914, she joined the Independent Labour Party (ILP).

During the war, Helen was a leading figure in the Red Clydeside Movement. In 1915 she led a mass movement against rent increases and evictions. Helen was chair of the South Govan Women's Housing Association and made efforts to win support from workers in the shipyards. She was also secretary of the Women's Peace Crusade and in July 1916, she organised an anti-war march of some 5,000 people.

In 1918 Helen was elected as Vice-chair of the Scottish ILP and she became a founder member of the ILP's left-wing which campaigned for affiliation to the Communist International. Crawford went to Moscow in 1920 for the Congress of the Third Communist International and interviewed Lenin. When the affiliation policy was defeated, she became a founder member of the Communist Party of Great Britain, within which she served on the Central Committee.

During the 1930s, Helen was a prominent member of the Friends of the Soviet Union. She was elected as Dunoon's first woman Town Councillor shortly after the war. Helen retired in 1947 due to poor health and died in 1954 aged 76.

Poem:
Lord Byron: Childe Harold's Pilgrimage
Canto 3, stanza 17

Lord Byron was a fierce opponent of militarism and war. In 1816 he visited the battlefield of Waterloo, not to join in with a wave of celebration and nationalism around the famous battle but to condemn the waste of life in the pursuit of 'king-making'. These lines are from his epic poem Childe Harold's Pilgrimage, published soon after his visit.

Childe Harold's Pilgrimage

Canto 3, stanza 17

Stop! – for thy tread is on Empire's dust!
An Earthquake's spoil is sepulchred below!
Is the spot mark'd with no colossal bust?
Nor column trophied for triumphal show?
None; but the moral's truth tells simpler so,
As the ground was before, thus let it be; –
How that red rain hath made the harvest grow!
And is this all the world has gained by thee,
Thou first and last of fields! king-making Victory?

23 April
Suffrage and socialism: Selina Cooper (1864-1946)

S elina was the daughter of a Cornish navvy.
When he died of typhoid fever, Selina's mother
took the family to find work in the textile mills
of northern England. Twelve-year old Selina
worked in the local textile mill at Barnoldswick.
She spent half the day in the factory and the other
half at school. At thirteen, Selina left school to
work full-time in the Barnoldswick Mill.
Selina joined the Nelson branch of the Cotton
Worker's Union. Although the majority of
members were women, the union was run by men.
Selina fought for the union to take up women's
issues. In 1891 she became involved in a trade
union dispute to force employers to provide decent
toilet facilities. Selina also demanded that the
union challenge the sexual harassment of women
workers.
Selina also began attending education classes
organised by the Women's Co-operative Guild
in Nelson. She read widely and studied medical
books so that she could help workers unable to
afford a visit to the doctors. Her book collection
included *The Law of Population*, a book written
by Annie Besant on birth-control.
In 1892 the Independent Labour Party (ILP)
was formed in Nelson and Selina joined. It was
at the local ILP that Selina met Robert Cooper, a
local weaver, committed socialist and advocate
of women's suffrage and they married in 1896.
Selina's first child, John Ruskin, who was named
after the writer she admired, died of bronchitis
when he was four months old. In 1900 Selina
Cooper joined the North of England Society for
Women's Suffrage. Other members at the time
included Esther Roper and Eva Gore-Booth.
Selina helped organize a petition by women
working in the Lancashire cotton mills. By spring
1901, 29,359 women from Lancashire had signed

the petition and Selina was chosen as one of the delegates to present the petition to the House of Commons.

That year, the ILP asked Selina to stand as a candidate for the forthcoming Poor Law Guardians. Although local newspapers campaigned against Selina, she became the first working woman to be elected as a Guardian. At the National Conference of the Labour Party in 1905, Selina urged the leadership to fully support women's suffrage. Selina developed a national reputation for her passionate speeches in favour of women's rights. In 1910 she was chosen to be one of the four women to present the case for women's suffrage to Herbert Asquith, the British Prime Minister.

In 1911 Selina Cooper became a national organiser for the NUWSS. Selina was behind the NUWSS decision in April 1912 to support Labour Party candidates in parliamentary by-elections. Selina's daughter later recalled how at a women's suffrage rally in Haworth, 'men threw rotten eggs and tomatoes and all sorts of things... we sheltered in a café. Mrs Aldersley went out and came back crying – covered with eggs and tomatoes... My mother went out, and she said, 'I'm stopping here, whatever you throw, so go and fetch all the stuff you've got to throw, because', she says, 'this blooming village would never have been known about but for three women - the Brontes'.'

Selina opposed the First World War and campaigned against military conscription. In 1917 Selina persuaded over a thousand women in Nelson to take part in a Women's Peace Crusade procession. The meeting ended in a riot and mounted police were called in to protect Selina and Margaret Bondfield, the two main speakers at the meeting. Selina was elected to the town council and became a local magistrate. In the 1930s she played a prominent role in the campaign against fascism. Selina died at home on 11 November, 1946 shortly before her eighty-second birthday.

Poem
Chris Searle's Poem for Blair Peach

 Forty-one years ago a young teacher from New Zealand, called Blair Peach was murdered by police on a demonstration against the Nazi National Front. Radical teacher Chris Searle wrote this poem for Blair, first published in *Socialist Worker* in April 1979.

Poem for Blair Peach

His was a precious, loving life.
He built his passion with great bridges
from the farthest islands of the southern seas
to the mist that clears in the classrooms of Bow –
Life was too short to stand injustice,
to stand the insults that he saw around him;
Human used as pawns
Humans named as the blame for the sorrow
that they themselves felt and lived!
He saw and lived oppression on his pulses –
Colours to him were beauty
not a form of self-made blindness!
The human is a beaming jewel,
from New Zealand to the streets of Southall
he shone with its brilliance!

You who seek to murder beauty – understand!
It rises with the dawn of every day
It stays and glows with the moon and the stars
It screams with the lungs of every new-born child
It reasons with the truth of every thinking human
–
Never forget the blood that crosses oceans,
Blair's brave heart swells to fill us all.

24 April
Socialists against Empire: Bhikaiji Rustom Cama (1861-1936)

B hikaiji Cama was born in Bombay (now Mumbai) into an affluent Parsi family. In 1885, she married Rustom Cama, a wealthy, pro-British lawyer, but the relationship did not prosper. In October 1896, Mumbai was hit by bubonic plague and Cama volunteered to provide care for the afflicted. She contracted the plague but survived and was sent to Britain for medical care in 1902. In London, Cama met a circle of radical opponents of British rule in India. She helped to set up the Indian Home Rule Society in 1905. She was banned from returning to India unless she signed a statement promising not to participate in nationalist activities. She refused. Cama moved to Paris where she co-founded the Paris Indian Society. Cama wrote, published and distributed revolutionary literature for the movement. In Paris, gave shelter to many revolutionaries, including Vladimir Lenin.

On 22 August 1907, Cama attended the second Socialist Congress at Stuttgart. Other delegates included Lenin, Rosa Luxemburg and Clara Zetkin. Cama gave a fiery speech, denouncing the effects of the British Raj and demanding equal rights and independence from Britain. She stunned the audience by unfurling an Indian flag, declaring, 'Behold, the flag of independent India is born! It has been made sacred by the blood of young Indians who sacrificed their lives in its honour. In the name of this flag, I appeal to lovers of freedom all over the world to support this struggle'.

Cama's flag, which she co-designed, became one template for the national flag of India. In 1909, Cama was involved in aiding the escape of a nationalist being deported to India to stand trial. The British government requested Cama's extradition, but the French government refused. The British government seized Cama's inheritance.

Bhikhaiji Cama actively supported the women's
suffrage movement and was vehement in her
support for gender equality. Speaking in Cairo,
Egypt, in 1910, she declared, 'I see here the representatives of only half the population of Egypt.
May I ask where is the other half? Sons of Egypt,
where are the daughters of Egypt? Where are your
mothers and sisters? Your wives and daughters?'
In 1914, France and Britain became allies, Cama
and other activists agitated among Indian troops
arriving in Marseilles on their way to the front.
Cama was told to leave Marseilles and 1915 she
was sent to Vichy, where she was interned. In
bad health, she was released in November 1917
and after the war, Cama returned to her home
in Paris. Cama remained exiled in Europe until
1935, when, gravely ill, she petitioned the British
government to be allowed to return home. She
finally agreed to renounce seditionist activities.
She died in Mumbai aged 74 on 13 August, 1936.

Delegates to the second Socialist Congress in Struttgart.
Rosa Luxemburg is in the centre, Bhikaiji possibly over on
right hand side.

Poem:
Claude McKay's If We Must Die

⭐ Claude McKay published 'If We Must Die' in July 1919. It was a protest against widespread racist attacks which took place that summer. The poem was published in *The Liberator*, run by Max and Crystal Eastman, and then Sylvia's Pankhurst's *The Workers' Dreadnought*. McKay was born in Jamaica but moved to America and became a key figure in the Harlem Renaissance where he wrote acclaimed, politically-committed poetry. He was a prominent fellow traveller of the Communist Party and visited Soviet Russia several times, receiving an ecstatic welcome. McKay also joined a militant union, The Industrial Workers of the World and helped to establish the radical African Blood Brotherhood. He lived in Britain from 1919 to 1920 where he worked with Sylvia Pankhurst to build international socialist organisation. In the mid-1930s, McKay became deeply critical of Stalinism. He converted to Catholicism and died of a heart attack in 1944 aged 58.

If We Must Die

If we must die, let it not be like hogs
Hunted and penned in an inglorious spot,
While round us bark the mad and hungry dogs,
Making their mock at our accursed lot.
If we must die, O let us nobly die,
So that our precious blood may not be shed
In vain; then even the monsters we defy
Shall be constrained to honor us though dead!
O kinsmen! we must meet the common foe!
Though far outnumbered let us show us brave,
And for their thousand blows deal one deathblow!
What though before us lies the open grave?
Like men we'll face the murderous, cowardly pack,
Pressed to the wall, dying, but fighting back!

25 April
Bolshevik Warrior: Evgenia Bosch (1875-1925)

Evgenia was born into an affluent Jewish family. At seventeen, her family tried to force her into an arranged marriage, but she ran off with Peter Bosh and had two daughters with him. Evgenia became a revolutionary socialist in 1901 aged 22 and joined the Bolsheviks in 1903. In 1906 she packed up her daughters, left a note for her husband and headed for Kiev, where she became secretary of the Russian Social Democratic Group. She was arrested and exiled to Siberia but escaped abroad, returning to Russia after the February Revolution. Evgenia became the leading Bolshevik in Ukraine. In October 1917, Bosch got permission to address a regiment of soldiers stationed in Ukraine. They were known as the Wild Division. Bosch spoke for two hours, explaining the need to replace the failing Provisional Government with a Soviet government. A month later the Chief of Staff wrote, 'Agitators, such as the Jewess Bosh, have contaminated all the units of the regiment'.
Shortly afterwards, another regiment stationed nearby in Vinnitsa mutinied. Bosch went to persuade the Wild Division not to obey their orders and crush the mutiny. The soldiers stood packed in a square in heavy rain and listened again. The next day she led them to join the mutineers and after a few days of fighting, the town of Vinnitsa fell to Bosch's rebels. The writer Victor Serge described of her as one of the most capable military leaders of the time. A few months later she launched the Ukrainian Congress of Soviets which announced a Soviet Republic. Evgenia became the first woman to lead a national government. After Lenin's death, she became a vocal critic of Stalin, and retired from active politics. In January 1925, devastated by the news that Trotsky had been forced out of his position as leader of the Red Army by Stalin, Evgenia committed suicide.

April 20
Against Racism, Against Empire: Catherine Impey (1847-1923)
& Ida B Wells (1862-1931)

Ida B Wells was born into slavery in Mississippi. Her family was freed by the Emancipation Proclamation during the American Civil War. Despite having to support her orphaned siblings from the age of sixteen, Ida trained as a teacher and co-owned the *Memphis Free Speech* which campaigned against racism and segregation. In 1890s, Ida exposed the horrors of lynching, which was used to oppress and intimidate African-American communities in the South. Her shocking reports reached the national press and her newspaper office was destroyed by racist mobs.

Ida moved to Chicago and in 1895 she married and had a family, but Ida did not let her family commitments stop her activism. On one occasion she was physically dragged off a train for refusing to give up her seat to a white person. She helped to set up the National Association for the Advancement of Colored People. In 1913, Ida set up the Alphra Suffrage Club to organise among Black women in Chicago. She also challenged racist female suffrage campaigners. When the National American Woman Suffrage Organisation organised a parade and demanded that Black women go to the back, Ida forced her way to the front.

During World War I, Ida was under government surveillance as a 'race agitator' and she worked with black leader Marcus Garvey to report on the race riots of 1919. Ida strongly supported workers' rights, urging all black women's organisations to sup-port the strikes of the Brotherhood of Sleeping Car Porters.

In 1893 Ida met an English woman, Catherine

Impey. Catherine was a radical Quaker who lived in Street, Somerset. In the 1870s, she travelled around America and was horrified by the racism she witnessed. Her small home became a meeting

place for Black activists including Frederick Douglass who visited her in 1888. After meeting Douglas, Catherine set up *Anti-Caste*, Britain's first anti-racist newspaper. *Anti-Caste* gave a platform to Black writers to expose racism and horrific working conditions within the British Empire. Catherine drew criticism for giving horrifying accounts of lynchings in the American South. Together Ida and Catherine set up a new organisation, The Society for the Recognition of the Universal Brotherhood of Man, which opposed racial segregation and lynching. Catherine invited Ida to tour England lecturing on lynching and racism. The two posted out 10,000 copies of *Anti-Caste* to build audiences for Ida's lecture tour. *Anti-Caste* failed when the British Anti-Lynching Society took over its main objective. Ida died in Chicago, in 1931, aged 68. Her autobiography, *Crusade for Justice*, was published

post-humously by her daughter. Catherine continued to campaign against war and injustice until her death in 1923.

Frederick
Douglas

Poem:
John Cornford: Poem

John Cornford was one of the first British volunteers for the Spanish civil war. Born in 1915, he was the son of the classicist, Francis Cornford and the poet, Frances Cornford. John Cornford joined the Young Communist League at the age of eighteen and became a full Party member at twenty. Newly graduated from Cambridge, with a 'starred' first and a brightly promising future, he left for Spain to fight for the Republican cause in August 1936 and joined the anti-Stalinist POUM (The Workers' Party of Marxist Unification). He fought in the battles for Madrid and Boadilla, and was killed on the Cordo-ba front in December, either on or just after his 21st birthday.

Poem

Heart of the heartless world,
Dear heart, the thought of you
Is the pain at my side,
The shadow that chills my view.

The wind rises in the evening,
Reminds that autumn is near.
I am afraid to lose you,
I am afraid of my fear.

On the last mile to Huesca,
The last fence for our pride,
Think so kindly, dear, that I
Sense you at my side.

And if bad luck should lay my strength
Into the shallow grave,
Remember all the good you can;
Don't forget my love.

27 April
Revolution Across Continents: Mika Feldman de Etchebéhère (1902-1992)

Mika was the child of Russian Jewish refugees who settled in Argentina. In 1920 while at university, she met Hipólito Etchebéhère, who became her compañero. They were involved in the Marxist-Anarchist group Insurrexit. They joined the Communist Party but were expelled for disagreeing with the leadership and supporting Trotsky. In 1931 they travelled to Spain, then in 1932 to Germany where they witnessed the rise of the Nazis, then to Paris, where they joined a revolutionary group, Que Faire. Three years later they returned to Spain where they joined a POUM, the anti-Stalinist militia set up to fight Franco. Mika was initially marginalised by the militia men who believed women should know their place. Mika replied, 'The women who are with us are militia members. We fight together, men and women, equal, and nobody better forget it! Mika fought so effectively alongside the men that she was made Captain and fought on the fronts of Sigüenza, Moncloa, Pineda de Húmera. Mika was also a member of Mujeres Libres (Free Women), an anarchist organisation set up in 1936 to fight for both women's liberation and social revolution with around 30,000 members. The wom-en challenged the dominant idea on the left that women should wait until after the revolution to fight for their liberation. During the Spanish Revolution, the Mujeres trained women in military skills so they could join the militias.

When the Republicans were defeated in 1939, Mika fled to France, but returned to Argentina before she could be arrested by Vichy. Mika returned to France in 1946. In Paris in 1968, Mika was seen getting students to wear gloves as they dug up paving stones to throw at the cops, so their hands would be clean and there would be no evidence against them. In 1975, she published a memoir of her time in Spain, *My war in Spain and Me.*

28 April
International Socialism and Anti-Fascism: Angelica Balabanoff (1878-1965)

Angelica Balabanoff was born to Jewish parents, in Kiev, Ukraine in 1878. She left home aged nineteen to study in Brussels, where she met Russian and Italian Marxists. After graduating, she continued to study under the Marxist philosopher, Antonio Labriola. She settled in Switzerland and became a lecturer and journalist for the Italian Socialist Party and party delegate to the Congresses of the Second International in 1907 and 1910.

In 1910, Angelica moved to Italy. She served on the Socialist Party's central committee and co-edited the party's paper, *Avanti*. She was a vocal opponent of World War I and was active in the anti-war Zimmerwald Movement. In 1917, she returned to Russia to support the revolution and was deeply moved by what she witnessed: 'You cannot form any idea of what is taking place here. One witnesses daily the miracle of reorganisation; one looks on at this work of constant renewal going on amidst attempts to boycott it, to sabotage and blockade it in all directions. The spectacle is infinitely inspiring; it fills you with pride; it revivifies your faith in human power and the divine potency of the ideal'. Angelica became secretary to the Communist International in 1919, working alongside Lenin and Trotsky. She opposed the measures they took to defeat the White Armies during the Civil War and left Russia, eventually settling in New York, where she campaigned to raise awareness of the danger represented by Benito Mussolini and Italian fascism. At the end of the Second World War, Angelica travelled once again to Italy and resumed her activity in Italian socialist politics. She died in Rome in 1965. In her memoir, *My Life as a Rebel,* Angelica wrote, 'The experience of over 40 years has only intensified my socialist convictions and if I had my life to live over again, I would dedicate it to the same objectives'.

Poem:
James Oppenheim: Bread and Roses

⭐ Bread and Roses originated in a speech given
by American women's suffrage and workers'
rights activist Helen Todd. The poem is associated
with the successful textile strike involving
many women immigrant workers in Lawrence,
Massachusetts in 1912, now often referred to as the
'Bread and Roses strike'.

As we come marching, marching, in the beauty of the day
A million darkened kitchens, a thousand mill-lofts gray
Are brightened by the beauty a sudden sun discloses
And the people hear us singing, "Bread and Roses, Bread and Roses."

As we come marching, marching, we battle, too, for men —
For they are in this struggle and together we can win
Our lives shall not be sweated from birth until life closes —
Hearts can starve as well as bodies: Give us Bread, but give us Roses

As we come marching, marching, a hundred million dead
Go crying through our singing their ancient cry for Bread;
Small art and love and beauty their grudging spirits knew —
It's Bread we fight for—but we fight for Roses, too

As we come marching, marching, we stand proud and tall —
The rising of the women is the rising of us all
No more the drudge and idler—ten that toil where one reposes —
But a sharing of life's glories: Bread and Roses, Bread and Roses
Bread and Roses

29 April
Disability and socialism: Helen Keller (1880-1968)

Keller is remembered as a powerful advocate for people with disabilities. She was also a suffra-gette, anti-war campaigner and revolutionary socialist. Helen was born in Tuscumbia, Alabama, to a confederate family. When she was nineteen months old, Helen contracted an illness which left her both deaf and blind. In 1886, she was referred to Alexander Graham Bell and went to an institute where she met Anne Sullivan, who became Keller's instructor and life-long companion. Helen joined the American Socialist Party in 1909 and by 1912 she had become a national voice for socialism. In 1913, Helen joined the militant Industrial Workers of the World (IWW) union. In an interview Helen explained her motivation: 'I was appointed on a commission to investigate the conditions of the blind. For the first time I, who had thought blindness a misfortune beyond human control, found that too much of it was traceable to wrong industrial conditions, often caused by the selfishness and greed of employers'.

Helen supported strikes against World War I and welcomed the Russian Revolution, writing articles in defence of Lenin and campaigning for an end to the blockade on Soviet Russia. She also campaigned tirelessly for the right of women to vote. In the 1930s, Helen became isolated from socialism although she never stopped campaigning for the disabled.

In 1911 Helen explained her commitment to socialism: 'The few own the many because they possess the means of livelihood of all ... The country is governed for the richest, for the corporations, the bankers, the land speculators, and for the exploiters of labor. The majority of mankind are working people. So long as their fair demands are set at naught, we can have neither men's rights nor women's rights'.

30 April
From women's suffrage to Stalin's Purges:
Rose Cohen (1884-1937) and Nellie Cohen (1886-1979)

The Cohen sisters were the daughters of Maurice and Ada Cohen, refugees from Poland who settled in Whitechapel in 1884. As teenagers, Rose and Nellie joined Sylvia Pankhurst's radical women's suffrage movement in East London. In 1913, Nellie became Sylvia Pankhurst's personal secretary. Nellie and Rose moved into a flat on Grays Inn Road with two comrades from the East London Federation of Suffragettes, Minnie Lansbury and May O'Callaghan. All four women in the flat became communists.

In March 1917, Sylvia addressed a meeting organised by the East London Jewish community to wel-come the overthrow of the Tsar. The Cohen sisters shared this enthusiasm for the Russian Revolution.

In 1919, Sylvia tried to set up a communist organisation from Nellie and Rose's flat and appointed Nellie to an organisation which built support for Soviet Russia. Rose became a prominent figure in the group, which won the approval of the Comintern, the Communist Party of Great Britain, founded in 1921.

In the 1920s and 1930s, Rose was entrusted with a series of missions for the Comintern, taking her to Paris, Moscow and Berlin. She met and married David Petrovsky, a Comintern agent, and in 1929 Rose gave birth to their son Alexey in Moscow, where she had settled. That same year, Nellie had a daughter, Joyce. The father was a married man who was unaware of Nellie's pregnancy. Nellie went live in New York's communist circles while she had the baby then she returned to England and worked in the Soviet Embassy in London.

Rose Cohen

In Moscow in the 1930s, Rose worked as the foreign editor of the USSR's only English-language newspaper, the *Moscow Daily News*. In the late 1930s, Stalin orchestrated a wave of arrests and executions. In 1937 Stalin's secret police came for Rose and David. He was arrested and executed in September. Rose was also arrested, distraught with fear about what would happen to her son. Prominent British communists such as Harry Pollitt appealed for her life, but Nellie failed to grasp the severity of her sister's situation. On 14 August, 1937, she wrote a letter to her sister filled with family anecdotes. The letter was returned to sender. Three months later, Rose was executed. Nellie remained a committed member of the Parliament Hill Fields branch of the Communist Party of Great Britain until her death in 1979.

1 May 20
Revolution, guns and peace: Anastasia Bitsenko (1875-1938)

A nastasia Bitsenko was born into a peasant family in a small village, but she managed to qualify as a teacher. During a famine in 1899, she organised communal kitchens before leaving for Moscow to continue her studies. There, she married Mikhail Bitsenko, a member of the Socialist Revolutionary Party. In 1901, they were arrested and banished for organising student disorders.
In 1903, Anastasia left her husband and travelled to St Petersburg, where she became a full-time activist for the Social Revolutionaries (SR). The next year, she joined a women's terrorist group which planned to assassinate a minister, but she was betrayed, arrested and exiled to the Arctic Circle. Anastasia escaped and returned to Moscow, where she was put in charge of organising rail workers before joining a SR flying combat detachment. In 1905 Anastasia volunteered to assassinate the Minister of War, who had brutally repressed a peasant revolt. She marched into his office, placed a draft of his death sentence on his desk and shot him dead. She was arrested and sentenced to death, but this was commuted to life imprisonment. She spent eleven years in penal servitude before being released by the February Revolution of 1917.
During the October Revolution, she served on the Petrograd Military Revolutionary Committee and the Central Executive Committee of the Soviets. Anastasia was appointed to the Soviet delegation to the Brest-Litovsk peace negotiations, which ended the fighting on the Eastern Front. Sitting amidst the uniformed generals Bitsenko stood out as the only women present, and almost certainly the only delegate who had shot a minister of war. Back in Russia in November 1918, she joined the Communist Party and served on several important committees. Anastasia fell victim to Stalin's purges. She was sentenced to death and shot on 16 June, 1938.

Poem for May Day: Voltairine de Cleyre (1866 – 1912)

 Voltairine de Cleyre was an American anarchist and feminist, a prolific writer and speaker who opposed religion, state power and capitalism, which she saw as interconnected with the op-pression of women. Her essay 'Sex Slavery' is a strikingly modern account of how gender ste-reotypes distorted women's lives. Her poem 'Hurricane' was inspired by a quote from August Spies one of the Haymarket Martyrs who was executed on trumped up charges after a riot on May Day, Chicago, 1886.

Hurricane
'We are the birds of the coming storm' — August Spies

The tide is out, the wind blows off the shore;
Bare burn the white sands in the scorching sun;
The sea complains, but its great voice is low.

Bitter thy woes, O People,
And the burden
Hardly to be borne!
Wearily grows, O People,
All the aching
Of thy pierced heart, bruised and torn!
But yet thy time is not,
And low thy moaning.
Desert thy sands!
Not yet is thy breath hot,
Vengefully blowing;
It wafts o'er lifted hands.

The tide has turned; the vane veers slowly round;
Slow clouds are sweeping o'er the blinding light;
White crests curl on the sea— its voice grows deep.

Angry thy heart, O People!
And its bleeding
Fire-tipped with rising hate!
Thy clasped hands part, O People,
For thy praying
Warmed not the desolate!
God did not hear thy moan:
Now it is swelling
To a great drowning cry;
A dark wind-cloud, a groan,
Now backward veering
From that deaf sky!

The tide flows in, the wind roars from the depths,
The whirled-White sand heaps with the foam-white waves;
Thundering the sea rolls o'er its shell-crunched wall!

Strong is thy rage, O People,
In its fury
Hurling thy tyrants down!
Thou metest wage, O People.
Very swiftly,
Now that thy hate is grown:
Thy time at last is come;
Thou heapest anguish,
Where thou thyself wert bare!
No longer to thy dumb.
God clasped and kneeling.
Thou answerest thine own prayer.

— Sea Isle City, New Jersey, August 1889

2 May
Racism, riot and unceasing revolt: Lucy Parsons (1851-1942)

Lucy Parsons was born in Virginia in 1851, the daughter of a slave. In 1863, she was moved to Texas where she worked as a seamstress and a cook for white families. In 1870, Lucy was living with a former slave, Oliver Gathing, and had a baby who died at birth. In 1871, Lucy married a white man, Albert Parsons. They were driven out of Texas by racists and settled in Chicago, Illinois.

Lucy began writing for *The Socialist* and *The Alarm*, the journal of the International Working People's Association. In the 1880s, she led marches of seamstresses in Chicago. On 4 May 1886, Albert addressed a rally at Haymarket Square, organised to protest against police violence during a May Day strike. Lucy was in the crowd when police moved in, a bomb was thrown at them and they shot several protesters dead. The authorities arrested eight men and, despite a lack of evidence, executed four activists. Albert was one of them. Protests against these judicial murders were beginning of May Day labour rallies in the US.

Lucy refused to be silenced. She spoke alongside William Morris and Peter Kropotkin during a visit to Great Britain in 1888. In the 1890s, she published *Freedom: A Revolutionary Anarchist-Communist Monthly*. In 1905 Lucy joined the syndicalist Industrial Workers of the World (IWW) union, and began editing *The Liberator*. She organized the Chicago Hunger Demonstrations in January 1915.

In the 1920s, the Chicago Police Department described Lucy as 'more dangerous than a thousand rioters'. In 1925 she worked with the National Committee of the International Labor Defense, a communist-led organization that defended labour activists and victimised black people. Historians believe that Lucy joined the Communist Party in 1939.

In her 80s, Lucy continued to speak out against capitalism. One of her last major appearances was in 1941 when she addressed striking workers at International Harvester. Lucy died on March 7, 1942, in house fire. Her lover,

"Never be deceived that the rich will permit you to vote away their wealth."

– Lucy Parsons

George Markstall, died the next day from injuries he received trying to save her. She was approximately 91 years old. After her death, police seized her 1,500 books. She is buried near her husband, near the Haymarket Martyrs' Monument in Forest Park, Illinois.

Poem
William Wordsworth on France (1794)

William
Wordsworth
was born 250
years ago.
Amidst the
official com-
memorations,
we should not
forget that
Wordsworth
was a radical
who travelled
to France in
1791 and was
inspired by
the vision of
revolutionary
change.

Oh! pleasant exercise of hope and joy!
For mighty were the auxiliars which then stood
Upon our side, we who were strong in love!
Bliss was it in that dawn to be alive,
But to be young was very heaven!—Oh! times,
In which the meagre, stale, forbidding ways
Of custom, law, and statute, took at once
The attraction of a country in romance!
When Reason seemed the most to assert her rights,
When most intent on making of herself
A prime Enchantress—to assist the work
Which then was going forward in her name!
Not favoured spots alone, but the whole earth,
The beauty wore of promise, that which sets
(As at some moment might not be unfelt
Among the bowers of paradise itself)
The budding rose above the rose full blown.
What temper at the prospect did not wake
To happiness unthought of? The inert
Were roused, and lively natures rapt away!
They who had fed their childhood upon dreams,
The playfellows of fancy, who had made
All powers of swiftness, subtilty, and strength
Their ministers,—who in lordly wise had stirred
Among the grandest objects of the sense,
And dealt with whatsoever they found there
As if they had within some lurking right
To wield it;—they, too, who, of gentle mood,
Had watched all gentle motions, and to these
Had fitted their own thoughts, schemers more wild,
And in the region of their peaceful selves;—
Now was it that both found, the meek and lofty
Did both find, helpers to their heart's desire,
And stuff at hand, plastic as they could wish;
Were called upon to exercise their skill,
Not in Utopia, subterranean fields,
Or some secreted island, Heaven knows where!
But in the very world, which is the world
Of all of us,—the place where in the end
We find our happiness, or not at all!

3 May
Revolutionary, republican and armed: Claire Lacombe (1765-?) and Pauline Leon (1768-1838)

Claire Lacombe was an actress but when she arrived in Paris in 1792, in the middle of the Great French Revolution, she left acting to become a revolutionary. Pauline was born to a family of Parisian chocolate makers and became a political radical after witnessing the execution of leaders of a bread riot.

Claire Lacombe

Like many working women, Claire and Pauline asserted their right to speak, to vote and to bear arms in defence of the Revolution. Pauline took part in the women's march to Versailles in 1789. During the insurrection of 10 August, 1792, they both took part in the storming of the Tuileries. Claire was shot through the arm but kept fighting and was awarded a medal for her courage.

Pauline Leon

In May, 1793, the two women united to set up the Society of Revolutionary Republican Women, the most radical female revolutionary organisation of the French Revolution. The society first acted as Jacobin Sans Culottes and then the more radical Enragés. They demanded that women be armed so they could defend the revolutionary republic and that women should have the right to vote in the councils of the Revolutionary Committee. Claire lived with Théophile Leclerc, leader of the Enrages, and supporter of women's rights. They broke up and Pauline married him. Under the Reign of Terror, the Enragés were suppressed, as was the Society of Revolutionary Republican Women. On 16 September, 1793, Claire was publicly denounced as a counter-revolutionary to the Committee of General Security. She was arrested and released in August 1795. She went back to the theatre but soon left and vanished into obscurity. In May 1794. Pauline and her husband were arrested and held separately in prison but later released. Pauline died at home on 5 October, 1838.

Poem:
William Blake: London (1794)

London

I wander thro' each charter'd street,
Near where the charter'd Thames does flow.
And mark in every face I meet
Marks of weakness, marks of woe.

In every cry of every Man,
In every Infants cry of fear,
In every voice: in every ban,
The mind-forg'd manacles I hear

How the Chimney-sweepers cry
Every blackning Church appalls,
And the hapless Soldiers sigh
Runs in blood down Palace walls

But most thro' midnight streets I hear
How the youthful Harlots curse
Blasts the new-born Infants tear
And blights with plagues the Marriage hearse

4 May
Suffragist, socialist, republican, communist: Charlotte Despard (1844-1939)

Charlotte French was born in Kent in 1844.
When she was ten her father died, and her
mother was committed to an asylum.
In 1870, Charlotte met and married Maximilian
Carden Despard. When he died in 1890, Charlotte
dedicated her life to fighting for socialism. In 1894
Charlotte was elected as a Poor Law Guardian in
Lambeth. She joined the Social Democratic Federation and later the Independent Labour Party. She
became friends with Eleanor Marx and was a delegate to the Second International in London in 1896.
Charlotte joined the Women's Social and Political
Union (WSPU). On 23 October, 1906, Charlotte
was arrested at the House of Commons. In 1907
she was imprisoned twice in Holloway Prison. She
also spent time in Ireland and in 1908 she helped
to form the Irish Women's Franchise League.
In 1909 she met Gandhi and, influenced by his
theory of passive resistance, Charlotte and 70 others left the WSPU to form the Women's Freedom
League (WFL). The WFL was militant but nonviolent. From 1912 to 1921, Charlotte had an intense,
relationship with Kate Harvey, a pacifist feminist.
Charlotte supported the workers during the Dublin
lock out of 1913. She was a tireless and coura-geous
opponent of World War I. In 1918, when women
finally won the vote, Charlotte became the Labour
Party candidate for Battersea but was defeated.
In 1920, Charlotte toured Ireland, collecting first-
hand evidence of atrocities and she helped to set up
the Women's Prisoners' Defence League to support
republican prisoners. Charlotte became involved in
the Sinn Fein campaign for a united Ireland.
In 1930 Charlotte joined the Communist Party and
became secretary of the Friends of Soviet Russia.
In her later years, she devoted her public speaking
to campaigns against fascism. Charlotte Despard
died on 10 November, 1939, after a fall in her new
house near Belfast.

5 May
Resistance, civil rights and stardom: Josephine Baker
(1906-1975)

Josephine Baker was born in St Louis. The identity of her father was never established. One of her grandparents was a former slave, the other of native American descent. At the age of twelve Josephine worked as a servant and a waitress, spending some time living rough on the streets. At fifteen, Josphine left for New York and started performing in clubs, the heart of the Harlem Renaissance.

In 1925, Josephine began performing in Paris, where she became a sensation and icon of the Jazz Age. She renounced her US citizenship and became a French national after her marriage to French industrialist Jean Lion in 1937. She raised her children in France. She aided the French Resistance during World War II, was awarded the Croix de guerre by the French military and was named a Chevalier of the Légion d'honneur by General Charles de Gaulle.

When the Civil Rights Movement emerged during the 1950s, Josephine became a supporter. On a visit to New York, she and her husband were refused reservations at 36 hotels and she wrote articles about segregation in the United States. She also began traveling into the South and giving talks on 'France, North Africa and the Equality of the Races in France'.

Josephine refused to perform for segregated audiences in the United States. Her insistence on mixed audiences helped to integrate live entertainment shows in Las Vegas. She received threat-ening phone calls from the Ku Klux Klan but said she was not afraid of them.

Josephine worked with the NAACP and was

presented with life membership. In 1963, she spoke at the March on Washington at the side of Rev. Martin Luther King Jr. While wearing her Free French uniform, she introduced the 'Negro Women for Civil Rights'. In her powerful speech, Josephine said: 'I have walked into the palaces of kings and queens and into the houses of presidents. And much more. But I could not walk into a hotel in America and get a cup of coffee, and that made me mad. And when I get mad, you know that I open my big mouth. And then look out, 'cause when Josephine opens her mouth,

they hear it all over the world.'

Josephine continued to perform throughout her life. On 8 April ,1975, Baker starred in a revue, celebrating 50 years in show business and won rave reviews. Four days later, Baker was found lying in bed. She died aged 68 on 12 April, 1975.

● You can see a clip of her in a film, *ZouZou* here: *https://youtu.be/XTrBlsBLXeg*

5 May
From celebrity Cinderella to communist:
Rose Pastor Stokes (1879-1933)

Rose Pastor Stokes was born into poverty, 'I slipped into the world while my mother was on her knees, scrubbing the floor', she later recalled. Born Rose Harriet Wieslander in Poland, 1879, she moved to England with her single mother when she was three. She lived in the slums of London's East End and started work at the age of eight. Her mother married Israel Pastor and they emigrated to Cleveland, USA. In 1890, Rose found work in a "buck-eye" (a cigar-sweatshop). Israel Pastor abandoned the family and Rose became the breadwinner for her mother and her four siblings. In 1901, she began contributing to *Yidishes Tageblat* (Jewish Daily News) and was employed as a columnist in New York City. She continued to write articles, plays and poems for the rest of her life. In one assignment Rose interviewed James Graham Phelps Stokes, a reform-minded millionaire. Their relationship caused a sensation. On 6 April 1905, the front page of the *New York Times* carried the headline 'J. G. Phelps Stokes to Wed Young Jewess', calling Rose the 'Cinderella of the sweatshops'.

In 1906, the couple joined the Socialist Party of America and Rose became a prominent public speaker. In 1909 Rose took part in the Shirtwaist Strike, known as the Uprising of the 20,000. In May and June 1912, she lead a strike by the New York City restaurant and hotel workers. Rose also distributed birth control information to working-class women.

Rose opposed the First World War and was arrested on 22 March, 1918, for an anti-war speech she gave in Kansas City, Missouri, in which she declared, 'No government which is for the profiteers can also be for the people, and I am for the people, while the government is for the profiteers'.

Rose became more radical than her millionaire husband and they divorced. She was a founder member of the Communist Party of American in 1919 and was elected to its Central Executive Committee, taking charge of the Women's Work Department. She was a delegate to the Comintern's Fourth World Congress in Moscow in 1922, where she submitted a minority report on the 'Negro question'.

In 1927, Rose remarried to a very different husband, Jerome Isaac Romain, a Russian-Polish Jewish communist. In 1929 she was arrested during a garment workers' strike. An activist in the poor Jewish area of New York's Lower East Side, Rose became known as 'Rose of the Ghetto'.

On 20 June, 1933 Rose died in Germany, where she had been treated for breast cancer. She was 53 years old. Rose had begun writing her autobiography in 1924 and she gave it to Samuel Ornitz, a communist writer who was to become a member of the blacklisted Hollywood Ten. Unfortunately, he never finished the book which was to have been called *I Belong to the Working Class*.

6 May
Princess mutineer: Rani Lakshmibai (1828-1858)

Rani Lakshmibai was born in 1828 into a rich Brahmin family. Rani married the Maharaja of Jhansi in May 1842. She gave birth to a boy in 1851. Her husband died in 1853 and the British East India Company, which ruled India, annexed the state. Rani was ordered to leave her palace. On 10 May, 1857 the Indian Rebellion, erupted. In June 1857, rebels seized the Fort of Jhansi and massacred 40 to 60 British officers. When the mutineers left Jhansi, Rani took over the city. She set up a foundry to cast cannon and assembled a military force to defend the city.

In March 1858 British forces arrived. When Commander Hugh Rose demanded the surrender of the city, Rani issued a proclamation: 'We fight for independence. In the words of Lord Krishna, we will if we are victorious, enjoy the fruits of victory, if defeated and killed on the field of battle, we shall surely earn eternal glory and salvation'. Sir Hugh Rose's forces besieged Jhansi in March 1858 and in April he launched an assault on the fort. Rani lead determined resistance to the British forces who had slaughtered men, women and children. Rani fled the city with her son and joined the mutineers occupying the city of Gwalior. When General Rose's forces attacked Gwalior in June, Rani again lead the resistance. British forces slaughtered 5,000 Indian soldiers and inflicted a decisive defeat on the rebels. Rani was killed by a British soldier.

Colonel Malleson wrote about Rani in his *History of the Indian Mutiny*: 'Whatever her faults in British eyes may have been, her countrymen will ever remember that she was driven by ill-treatment into rebellion, and that she lived and died for her country'.

7 May
Mary Shelley (1797-1851)

Mary Shelley was the daughter of the radical philosopher William Godwin and the famous feminist, Mary Wollstonecraft, who died just days after Mary's birth. Mary grew up with five semi-related siblings in an unconventional but intellectually electric household.

At the age of sixteen, Mary eloped to Italy with the poet Percy Bysshe Shelley. Each encouraged the other's writing, and they married in 1816 after the suicide of Shelley's wife. They had four children, tragically only one survived.

In 1816, when she was just twenty, Mary took part in a ghost-writing competition on a stormy night with Lord Byron at Lake Geneva. Mary wrote *Frankenstein*, the first true work of science-fiction and powerful exploration of the destructive nature of power when allied to wealth.

After Percy Shelley drowned in 1822, Mary returned to London and pursued a very successful career as a novelist, biographer and editor of Shelley's poetry, which would not have been published without her. She was also a single mother, constantly battling Shelley's wealthy but conservative family to protect his radical legacy. Mary did not abandon the radicalism she had shared with Shelley, as many have suggested. Mary was a lifelong reformer and feminist. She supported all European revolutionary movements and wrote articles for Leigh Hunt's radical periodical *The Liberal*. She also corresponded with abolitionist and feminist Frances Wright, who invited her to join her utopian community in Tennessee.

Mary had affairs with women. Writing to her close friend in 1835, Mary recalled her loneliness saying: 'I was so ready to give myself away – and being afraid of men, I was apt to get tousy-mousy for women.' (Tousy-mousy was sexual slang for vagina.)

Her novels, such as *Lodore* and *Falkner*, had strongly feminist plots. *Valperga* was a feminist, republican version of Walter Scott's historical novels and her works often argued that women were the ways to reform civil society. Mary died aged just 54.

Her poem 'Ode to Ignorance' (1834) is a scathing account of how the tyrannies of her day are sustained by military might and ideological control. She calls for hope in possibilities of change. It is as powerful and militant as the brilliant poems written by her husband. This is an excerpt, but you can read whole version here: *https://allpoetry.com/Mary-Wollstonecraft-Shelley*

Ode to Ignorance

Hail, Ignorance! majestic queen!
Mysterious, mighty, dark, profound in mien!
Sprung from no upstart brood of Light,
But of the ancient house of Night!
Daughter of that stupendous line,
Which ere the base-born Sun did shine,
Or one plebeian star appear'd,
Their awful throne in chaos rear'd —
The old nobility of Hell,
Who through the realms of darkness wide,
With lordly morgue and feudal pride
Did reign, and when imperial Satan fell,
By rebel cherubim cast down
And robb'd of his ancestral crown,
Received him like a Bourbon there.
With fond aristocratic care.

Hail! bounteous mother of each royal race;
Corruption, Bigotry, and Fraud,
Reflect thy dim patrician face;
They many a kingdom fair and broad,
Great Ignorance, receive from thee —
Thou who didst take the World in fee!
Ay! thou dost call the total earth thy own;
And every tyrant for his throne
Doth homage at thy knee!

Thou dost for kings, in dungeons bind
The anarch Truth, the rebel Mind,
Who never slip their iron bolts
But some fair realm revolts,
All hail! Legitimacy's star!
Protectress of the despot Czar!
Thee Czars invoke, and, gorged with Polish blood,
Hallow thy name, and style thee great and good!
Night of the Mind, how long, how long,
Thy praise hath blazoned been in song!
Hail! mighty, mighty queen!
August ! Serene!
Peers are thy children-noble peers!
Thou sucklest them upon thy breasts;
Thine is their youth, and thine their years.
Transfus'd on them, thy ample spirit rests:
Night of the Mind! all hail!
Gloomy and grand,
Through every land,
Great queen! dost thou prevail!
...

But, hah! what hideous change is this?
What damn'd magician interrupts thy bliss?
The eye-ball aches,
And flashes on the sight a horrid gleam
Alas, His Day that breaks!
'Tis orient knowledge darts that baleful beam —
Knowledge, thy dauntless foe!
Where wilt thou fly, how shun the blow?
What work, what palisade behind?
Night of the mind!
Thy sons are stricken with dismay;
They cannot bear
The hateful glare,
But curse the name of Day.
Prelates wake who long have slumber'd,
Peers believe their days are number'd,
Priests before their altars tremble,
Courtiers shudder, kings dissemble,
Pensioners and place-men quake,
All the sons of rapine shake;

Guillotines are lordly themes,
Barricades haunt royal dreams,
Bigots frighted to their souls,
Shrink into their narrow holes,
To den of filth corruption steals,
Reform fierce-barking at his heels,
All expect disastrous doom,
All the things that love the gloom,
All that crouch, and skulk, and prowl,
Wolf and tiger, bat and owl;
Yet still to thee, their bounteous patroness,
They lift adoring eyes;
And none apostatize,
Nor aught the less
Thy name they bless,
Because thy kingdom hath been rudely torn,
And of a mist or two thy stupid skull been shorn.
Oh! for thy loyal sons
Hast thou no guerdon fair, no just reward?
No new resource,
No untried force,
To save them from their foe abhorr'd?
Come with a host of Huns!
Unlock once more thy garners of the North:
Unleash the Goth and send the Vandal forth;
Exert thy waning might;
Rally the powers of Night;
Renew the desp'rate fight!
Tat tyrants may rebuild thy mouldering fanes:
So may'st hope,
Loading thy foes with slavery's ponderous chains,
With holy, heavenly light, triumphantly to cope!

8 May
The most dangerous woman in America:
Mary 'Mother' Jones (1837-1933)

Mary Harris was born in 1837 in County Cork, Ireland. Her father, Robert, fled to Canada after taking part in a revolt against local landowners. Mary became a schoolteacher but was barred from most schools because she was a Roman Catholic. She later moved to Chicago and worked as a dressmaker. In 1861, she met George Jones, an ironworker and union organiser, and they married and had four children. George and the four children, all under five years old, died in a yellow fever epidemic in Memphis in Autumn 1867.

After the death of her family, Mary moved back to Chicago and to dressmaking but in 1871 she lost her home, shop, and belongings in the Great Chicago Fire. After the fire she became a full-time organiser for the Knights of Labor. In the 1880s Mary left the Knights to become a strike organiser. In 1901, Mary was involved in a significant strike in Pennsylvania's silk mills, involv-ing a workforce of teenage women who demanded adult wages. Mary encouraged the families of the workers to beat on tin pans, and shout 'join the union!'

In 1902 Mary was arrested and put on trial for ignoring an injunction banning meetings by strik-ing miners. 'There sits the most dangerous woman in America', announced the district attor-ney, "She comes into a state where peace and prosperity reign ... crooks her finger [and] twenty thousand contented men lay down their tools and walk out.' The following year, Mary organ-ised children from the mills and mines to join a 'Children's Crusade', in which the children marched from Kensington, Philadelphia to the hometown of President Theodore Roosevelt car-rying banners which demanded 'We want to go to school and not the mines!'

Mary, who was now in her 50s, became known as Mother Jones. In 1905, she was among the founders of the Industrial Workers of the World (the Wobblies). She was also a founding member of the Social Democratic Party in 1898.

During the 1912 Paint Creek Cabin strike in West Virginia, Mary organised workers despite a shooting war between United Mine Workers members and the private army employed by the mine owners. Martial law was declared and Mother Jones was arrested on 13 February, 1913 and brought before a military court. Accused of conspiring to commit murder, she refused to recognize the legitimacy of her courtmartial. She was sentenced to twenty years in the state penitentiary but was moved to house arrest and released due to ill health.

She helped organize coal miners in Colorado in the 1913-1914 United Mine Workers of America strike against the Rockefeller-owned Colorado Fuel and Iron company, in what became known as the Colorado Coalfield War. Again, she was arrested and served time in prison. Jones was a union organizer for the United Mineworkers Union into the 1920s and continued to give fiery speeches. One of her last public appearances was at her birthday celebration on 1 May, 1930. She died a few months later and buried at the Miners Cemetery at Mount Olive, Illinois: It was the only cemetery owned by a union.

10 May
A revolutionary in her own right: Inessa Armand (1874-1920)

nessa Armand was born in Paris in 1874, the daughter of a French opera singer and a Russian aristocrat. She was brought up by her Russian grandmother in Moscow. She married a rich French Russian, Alexander Armand, at the age of nineteen and had four children. In 1901, she was refused permission by the Moscow authorities to open a school for girls. The following year she opened a shelter for 'downtrodden women'. At the age of twenty-eight, Inessa left Alexander and went to live with his younger brother Vladimir, who was a revolutionary, and had a child with him. In 1903 she joined the Russian Social Democratic and Labour Party (RSDLP) and began to work in the underground movement. For the next fifteen years she tried to combine her political life with raising her children. She smuggled documents across the border from Switzerland into Russia in the false bottom of her children's trunk. In Moscow during the 1905 revolution, Inessa was arrested but released thanks to Alexander's intercession. She was arrested again in April 1907 and exiled to northern Russia in November. She escaped a year later and hurried to Switzerland to nurse Vladimir, who died two weeks later. Armand then travelled to Paris, where she first met Krupskaya and Lenin. She was to share the next seven years of exile with them. Inessa taught at a party school in Geneva in 1911 alongside Lenin, Zinoviev and Kamenev. She also became the main organiser of the committee that coordinated all the Bolshevik groups across Europe. She returned to Russia in 1912 and was arrested. Again she escaped, but not before she helped to steer the Bolshevik Party's paper towards addressing women workers. Inessa was also the driving force behind the Bolshevik's women's paper *Rabotnitsa*.

Inessa opposed World War I, organising anti-war conferences and publications.

During the Russian Revolution of 1917, Inessa became secretary to the Moscow Soviet and pushed through reforms which benefitted women. She was vital to establishing the first Congress for working women in 1918. From this congress the Women's Department, or Zhenotdel, was set up, enabling Inessa to organise communal facilities such as laundries, canteens and crèches. She launched a paper aimed at women, *Kommunista*, but the fifth edition carried her own obituary. Exhausted by working sixteen-hour days she went to recuperate at a sanatorium in the Caucasus Mountains. She was evacuated when the area came under attack by White armies, and when she left the train to buy bread and milk Inessa contracted cholera. She died on 23 September, 1920, aged 46. She was buried in Red Square with mass singing of the Internationale; one of

very few women of the time to be accorded a state funeral.

The year before she died Inessa wrote: 'All the interests of women workers, all the conditions for their emancipation are inseparably connected to the victory of the proletariat, are unthinkable without it. But this victory is unthinkable without their participation, without their struggle'.

Inessa with her children

11 May　　Thanks Lesley M. Atkins
Labour Movement Martyrs and their Stories:
Ella May Wiggins (1900-1929) **& Mary Heaton** (1874-1966)

Ella May Wiggins

Ella May was born in Sevierville, Tennessee, in 1900 and by 1926 she had settled in an African-American neighbourhood in Gaston County. Her neighbours looked after her nine children when she went to work as a spinner at American Mill No. 2. She worked twelve-hour days, six days a week, earning about nine dollars a week.

Ella May became a bookkeeper for the commu-nist-led union. She travelled to Washington DC, to testify about labour practices in the South, giving a powerful testimony: 'I'm the mother of nine. Four died with the whooping cough, all at once. I was working nights, I asked the super to put me on days, so's I could tend 'em when they had their bad spells. But he wouldn't. I don't know why. ... So I had to quit, and then there wasn't no money for medicine, and they just died'.

Mary Heaton

Ella May sang ballads, including her best-known song, 'A Mill Mother's Lament', which was recorded by Pete Seeger. She organised African-American workers alongside whites, and her local NTWU branch was one of few to admit African-Americans to the union.

On 14 September, 1929, she and other union members drove to a union meeting in Gastonia, North Carolina. They were met by an armed mob and turned back. They had driven about five miles toward home when they were stopped by a car; armed men jumped out and began shooting. Ella May was shot in the chest and killed. In March 1930, five Loray Mill employees were charged with her murder but were acquitted after a trial which lasted less than thirty minutes, despite fifty wit-nesses. Her surviving children sent to orphanages. Ella May was buried in the Bessemer City Cemetery with a gravestone inscribed, 'She died carrying the torch of social justice'. Three of her children were later buried near her.

■ Ella May Wiggins life and death was fictionalised in *Strike!* a 1930 work by Mary Heaton Vorse, another labour activist and socialist.

Mary Heaton was born 11 October, 1874, in New York City. She left school and spent time in Paris studying art. In 1896 she married her first husband, journalist Albert White Vorse. She had two children and began campaigning for women's rights in October 1898.

In 1904, the Vorses moved to Venice, where Mary was first introduced to labour struggles. Bert died in 1910 and Mary married another journalist, Joe O'Brien, a socialist she met during the 1912 Lawrence Textile Strike. The couple had one child who died a year later.

Mary Heaton Vorse (left) and fellow activists prepare to leave to provide food for striking miners in Kentucky in 1932

Mary campaigned against World War I and was a founding member of the Woman's Peace Party in January 1915. She was the delegate of the New York Woman Suffrage Party to an International Women's Peace Congress.

Mary wrote for many left-wing newspapers, including Crystal Eastman's *The Masses* and wrote several novels, including *Strike!* Mary participated in and reported on the Lawrence Textile Strike, the steel strike of 1919, the textile workers strike of 1934, and coal strikes in Harlan County, Kentucky.

From 1919 to 1923, Mary was in a relationship with the radical political cartoonist and Communist Party functionary Robert 'Fighting Bob' Minor. Mary died in 1966 aged 92.

● You can hear Pete Seeger singing 'A Mill Mother's Lament' here *https://www.youtube. com/watch?v=Q69onG2nXtg&feature=youtu.be*

12 May
'We are Lions': Jayaben Desai (1933-2010)

Jayaben Desai was born in 1933 in Gujarat, India. She later migrated to Britain, where she took up low-paid work, first as a sewing machinist, then processing film in the Grunwicks factory. No trade unions were allowed to organise at Grunwicks, where the white management con-trolled the workers through threats, racist insults and harassment. On 20 August 1976, Mrs De-sai, and her son, Sunil, walked out in protest. Her parting words to the manager were, 'What you are running here is not a factory, it is a zoo. But in a zoo there are many types of animals. Some are monkeys who dance on your finger-tips, others are lions who can bite your head off. We are those lions, Mr Manager'.

Outside she joined four other workers who had left earlier that day in protest at conditions. To-gether, the six workers joined the APEX union and started picketing the factory. Soon there were 137 workers on strike, protesting about the conditions at Grunwicks and calling for union recognition.

The strikers launched a campaign to win solidarity from other workers, from engineering facto-ries in Glasgow to the coalmines of south Wales. On Monday 13 June, 1977, the police arrested 84 pickets out of 100 who had come to demonstrate their solidarity on what was called Women's Support Day.

The following Friday there were 1,300 pickets and numbers swelled to 12,000 by 11 July, the day that 20,000 went on a TUC-organised march to the factory. The Cricklewood postal workers took sol-idarity action, blacking the Grunwicks mail. Colin Maloney, their leader, observed: 'You don't say 'no' to Mrs Desai.' The postal workers, who were most-ly white, were suspended for three weeks.

The government used the law to crush the striker and the union leaders betrayed them. When Jaya-ben was suspended by her own union, she rightly

observed that, 'the union views itself like management. There's no democracy there'.

Defiant to the end, Jayaben told the final meeting of the strikers that they could be proud. 'We have shown', she said, 'that work-ers like us, new to these shores, will never accept being treated without dignity or respect. We have shown that white workers will support us'. Only ten years previously, dockers had marched in support of the racist Conserv-ative politician Enoch Powell but the Grunwicks dispute witnessed the biggest mobilisation in British labour-movement history in support of fewer than 200 mainly Asian women strikers.

Jayaben Desai died in 2010 aged 77.

13 May
Poet, wit, radical: Dorothy Parker (1893-1967)

orothy Rothschild was born in 1893, New Jersey, US, the child of Jacob Henry Rothschild and his wife Eliza Annie. Her mother died a month before Dorothy's fifth birthday. Following her father's death in 1913, she played piano at a dancing school to earn a living while she worked on her poetry. In 1917, she met a Wall Street stockbroker, Edwin Pond Parker.

Dorothy's career took off in 1918 when she was writing theatre criticism for *Vanity Fair* establishing a national reputation as a wit and poet. Her first volume of poetry, *Enough Rope*, was published in 1926 and sold 47,000 copies. Parker divorced her husband in 1928 and had several affairs. When she fell pregnant Dorothy is alleged to have said, 'how like me, to put all my eggs into one bastard'. She had an abortion and fell into a depression that culminated in her first attempt at suicide.

In 1932, Dorothy married actor Alan Campbell and together they moved to Hollywood.

In 1934 Dorothy and Alan wrote the script for the 1937 film *A Star Is Born* and were nominated for an Academy Award for Best Writing. She contributed dialogue for another film *The Little Foxes* in 1941. The screenplay was written by Lillian Hellman, who was later blacklisted by Hollywood for her Communist sympathies.

Dorothy's lifelong commitment to political activism began in 1927 when she protested against the executions of Sacco and Vanzetti, Italian immigrants and anarchists who were unjustly executed for murder. During the protest in Boston, Dorothy was arrested and fined. She claimed that from then on 'my heart and soul are with the cause of socialism'.

During the 1930s and 1940s, Parker became a vocal supporter of radical causes. In 1937, she went to Spain and reported from the Republicans side for the communist magazine, *The New Masses*. She also wrote an impressive short-story, *Soldiers of the Republic*.

Dorothy helped to set up the Hollywood Anti Nazi League in 1936, working alongside Otto Katz, a Soviet Comintern agent, and German communist Willi Münzenberg. Dorothy served as chair of the Joint Anti-Fascist Refugee Committee's fundraising arm, 'Spanish Refugee Appeal'. She organised Project Rescue Ship to transport Republican fighters to safety in Mexico and headed up the Spanish Children's Relief Fund.

Dorothy made donations to the National Association for the Advancement of Colored People (NAACP), the Abraham Lincoln Brigade, a battalion of black volunteers fighting Franco's fascists. This battalion included black poet Langston Hughes. She also wrote articles on injustice.

During these years, Dorothy described herself as a communist and she was listed as a communist by the publication *Red Channels* in 1950. The FBI compiled a 1,000-page dossier on her because of her involvement in communism. Studio bosses placed her on the Hollywood blacklist. Her final screenplay was *The Fan*, a 1949 adaptation of Oscar Wilde's play *Lady Windermere's Fan*, directed by Otto Preminger.

Her marriage to Campbell was tempestuous. They divorced in 1947, remarried in 1950, then separated in 1952. Campbell died from a drug overdose in 1963. Dorothy died of a heart attack on 7 June, 1967, at the age of 73. In her will, she bequeathed her estate to Martin Luther King Jr. Following King's death, her estate was bequeathed by his family to the National Association for the Advancement of Coloured People.

14 May
The Red: Louise Bryant (1885-1936)

L ouise Bryant grew up in rural Nevada and attended the Universities of Nevada and Oregon. In 1909 she graduated with a degree in history and married Paul Trullinger. She became a journalist and an activist in the women's suffrage movement. In 1915, she met John Reed, left her first husband, and moved with Reed to Greenwich Village. They worked together on a socialist newspaper, *The Masses*, and married in 1916.

In August 1917, Louise and John managed to get themselves assigned to report from the Russian Revolution. They arrived in Petrograd in time to witness the October Revolution. They attended gatherings at the Smolny Institute and interviewed many leading political figures, including Lenin, Trotsky, and Kerensky, and both eventually published books—*Six Red Months in Russia* by Bryant and Reed's *Ten Days That Shook the World*. Louise covered Duma meetings, dining in public mess halls with soldiers and workers, and interviewing women revolutionaries, such as Maria Spiridonova and Alexandra Kollontai, who was the only woman in the Bolshevik cabinet. By the time she returned to New York, her vivid accounts of the revolution were being read across North America.

Louise arrived in New York in 1918. The US government had forced *The Masses* to shut down, but Bryant wrote articles about the October Revolution for other publications and gave public meetings urging support for the revolution.

In October, Bryant's *Six Red Months in Russia*, was published giving an inspirational account of how the revolution transformed every aspect of life. In February 1919, Louise went to Washington, DC, to speak about Russia. She participated in a National Woman's Party suffrage rally, during which she was arrested, charged, and sentenced to five days in jail.

The story of Bryant, Reed and the Russian Revolution is told in the 1981 film *Reds,* starring Diane Keaton as Bryant and Warren Beatty as Reed.

You can read Louise's brilliant book on *Marxist. org.uk*

Louise testified in front of the Overman Committee, which investigated Bolshevik activity in the US. Soon afterwards, she began a cross-country speaking tour, The Truth About Russia, during which she addressed large audiences in Detroit, Chicago, Spokane, Seattle, San Francisco and Los Angeles. Louise was the first woman to defend Lenin and Trotsky and demand Hands Off Russia at political gatherings across the US.

The US government outlawed the American Communist Party. In danger of being arrested and unable to get a passport to go to Russia, John Reed disguised himself as a stoker and left the US in late September 1919. During the Palmer Raids, John was charged with conspiring to overthrow the US government by force. In March 1920, he was arrested while returning home through Finland and was then returned to Moscow in a prisoner exchange. He cabled Bryant, Passport home refused. Temporarily returning headquarters. Come if possible. Traveling without passport. Bryant, disguised as the wife of a Swedish businessman, arrived in Petrograd in late August 1920. She arrived in time to be at John's side when he died of typhus.

She returned to the US in mid-summer 1921, and married William Bullitt, Jr, a wealthy film maker. Louise returned to Russia to write portraits of leading political figures, which led to her second book, *Mirrors of Moscow*, published in 1923.

Later in 1923, Bryant and Bullitt moved to Paris. Two months later, Bryant gave birth to her only child, Anne Moen Bullitt. In 1925 she and Bullitt adopted an eight-year-old Turkish boy.

By 1926, Louise was suffering from a painful disease and was drinking heavily. Bullitt accused her of having a lesbian affair and divorced her, winning sole custody of Anne. Bryant remained in Paris, occasionally advising the writer and communist Claude McKay.

Louise died near Paris on 6 January, 1936, of a brain haemorrhage.

15 May

Black Liberation: Assata Shukar (1947-)

JoAnne Byron was born in Flushing, Queens, and grew up in New York City. She became involved in political activism at Borough of Manhattan Community College and City College of New York. After graduating in 1971, JoAnne moved to Oakland, California and joined the Black Panther Party. She organised protests and community education programmes. After returning to New York City, Shakur led the Panther chapter in Harlem, coordinating the Free Breakfast Program for children.

She left the Panthers and joined the Black Liberation Army (BLA), whose members drew inspiration from the Vietcong, and led a campaign of terrorist activities against the US government. She began using the name Assata Olugbala Shakur in 1971, rejecting JoAnne Chesimard as a 'slave name'. She now identified as an African.

Between 1971 and 1973, Assata was charged with several crimes and was the subject of a multi-state manhunt. In May 1973, she was arrested after being wounded in a shootout on the New Jersey Turnpike in which a state trooper was shot dead. Between 1973 and 1977, Assata was charged with murder, attempted murder, armed robbery, bank robbery, and kidnapping in relation to the Turnpike Shootout and six other incidents. She was acquitted on three of the charges and three were dismissed. In 1977, Assata was convicted of the murder of the state trooper and of seven other felonies related to the shootout.

Assata was treated appallingly in prison. She was continuously confined in a men's prison and left without adequate food and exercise. Assata was identified as a political prisoner in 1973 by Angela Davis, and again in 1977, by the *New York Times*. International investigators cited Assata's treatment as 'one of the worst cases' of prison abuse and described her as a victim of the FBI, who had terrorised black activists with false arrests, entrapment, fabrication of evidence, and spurious criminal prosecutions.

On 2 November, 1979, she escaped from the Clinton Correctional Facility for Women, when three members of the Black Liberation Army visiting her drew concealed .45-caliber pistols and a stick of dynamite, seized two correction officers as hostages, and commandeered a van.

After her escape, Shakur lived as a fugitive and was protected by her community. The FBI circulated wanted posters throughout New York. In response her supporters hung 'Assata Shakur is Welcome Here' posters. In New York, three days after her escape, more than 5,000 demonstrators carried signs with the same slogan. In July 1980, FBI director William Webster admitted that the search for Assata had been frustrated by residents' refusal to cooperate.

Assata did not surface until 1984 when she was granted political asylum in Cuba. She has lived in Cuba since, despite US government efforts

to have her returned. She is still on the FBI Most Wanted Terrorists list, as JoAnne Deborah.

16 May
Striking a Light: Sarah Chapman (1862-1945)

Sarah was born in 1862 to Samuel Chapman, a brewer and sometime docker, and Sarah Ann Mackenzie. Sarah and her six siblings grew up in Mile End and could all read and write, which was unusual for the time.

By the age of nineteen, Sarah worked with her mother and sister, Mary, at the Bryant and May match factory in Bow. The match women were known for being rowdy and rebellious. They were mainly of Irish descent and were familiar with republican and socialist ideas. In 1882, factory boss, Theodore Bryant, deducted a shilling from each worker's wage to pay for a statue of Liberal prime minister William Gladstone. Workers disrupted the unveiling by pelting the statue with stones and red paint and cutting their fingers to smear the statue in their own blood.

Anger among the women was fuelled by low wages, long hours, appalling working conditions and the unfair fines system. Poisonous white phosphorus left many girls suffering from 'phossy jaw', a disfiguring and agonising form of cancer. In July 1888, some 1,400 women marched out of the factory after a woman was sacked. The next day some 200 girls marched from Mile End down to see Annie Besant, a campaigning journalist. A deputation of three, including Sarah, went into her office and Annie agreed to help them organise a Strike Committee to which Sarah and eight other women were elected.

The first strike meeting was followed by meetings with Members of Parliament. The women marched from the East End into central London to win support and went from door to door collecting solidarity donations.

By 17 July, their demands were met. All fines and deductions were abolished and all sacked workers were reinstated. Bryant and May provided a room for meals away from the poisons of the work room. The Union of Women Match Makers was set at Stepney Meeting Hall, and twelve women, including Sarah, were elected to its committee. Sarah was elected by her union to be the first TUC representative and she was also a delegate to the 1888 International TUC in London.

In December 1891, Sarah married Charles Henry Dearman, a cabinet maker, and stopped working at Bryant and May. They moved to Bethnal Green and had six children.

Sarah died of lung cancer, in Bethnal Green in 1945 aged 83. The Match women should be remembered as a collective of powerful and insurgent women whose victory helped to inspire the Great Dock Strike of 1889.

■ Read more in Louise Raw's great book *Striking a Light: The Match Women's Place in History* is available from Bookmarks: *https://bookmarks-bookshop.co.uk*

17 May
From terrorism to Marxist revolutionary:
Vera Ivanovna Zasulich (1851-1919)

Vera Zasulich was born in Mikhaylovka, in the Russian Empire, the daughter of an impoverished minor noble. After graduating from high school in 1866, she moved to St Petersburg and worked as a clerk. She became involved in radical politics and taught literacy classes for factory workers. She was just seventeen when she was arrested and imprisoned for four years in 1869.

Vera was released in 1873, she settled in Kiev, where she became a leader of a revolutionary group of Mikhail Bakunin's anarchist supporters. In July 1877, a political prisoner, Alexei Bogolyubov, refused to remove his cap in the presence of Colonel Trepov, the governor of St. Petersburg who was famous for his suppression of rebellions. Trepov ordered Bogolyubov to be flogged, which caused outrage. A group of revolutionaries plotted to kill Trepov and Vera was selected to act. She walked calmly into his office and shot and seriously wounded Trepov. At her widely publicized trial, it was Trepov's crimes which were put on trial and the jury found Zasulich not guilty. Vera fled the court as the police tried to rearrest her. A crowd gathered to protect her and one of her supporters was shot dead. In the chaos, Vera managed to escape. Vera fled to Switzerland, where she became a Marxist and co-founded the Emancipation of Labour group with Georgi Plekhanov and Pavel Axelrod in 1883. The group commissioned Zasulich to translate Karl Marx's key works into Russian and these texts were the basis of the creation of the Russian Social Democratic Labour Party (RSDLP) in 1898.

In mid-1900, the leaders of the radical wing of the new generation of Russian Marxists, Julius Martov, Vladimir Lenin and Alexander

Potresov, joined Zasulich, Plekhanov and Axelrod in Switzerland. The six founded *Iskra*, a revolutionary Marxist newspaper, and formed its editorial board.

The *Iskra* editors convened a pro-Iskra Second Congress of the RSDLP in Brussels and London in 1903. The *Iskra* supporters split into two factions, Lenin's Bolsheviks and Martov's Mensheviks and Vera sided with the Mensheviks.

She returned to Russia after the 1905 Revolution and joined a group with Plekhanov in early 1914. The group supported their own government in World War I and opposed the October Revolution of 1917. In the winter of 1919, Vera developed pneumonia and died in Petrograd on 8 May 1919. In his book *Lenin*, Leon Trotsky acknowledged her contribution to Russian socialism: 'She remained to the end the old radical intellectual on whom fate grafted Marxism. Zasulich's arti-cles show that she had adopted to a remarkable degree the theoretic elements of Marxism. But the moral political foundations of the Russian radicals of the '70s remained untouched in her until her death'.

● Postscript: The first play Oscar Wilde wrote

was *Vera; or, The Nihilists*, inspired by Vera's shooting of General Trepov. The play was published in 1880 and first performed in New York in 1883.

18 May
Agitating for reform: Ernestine Louise Rose (1810-1892)

Ernestine Potowska was born in Poland. Her father was a wealthy Rabbi. When she was sixteen, her father betrothed her to an older man. Rose rejected the match and took the unusual step of appealing to a secular civil court which ruled in her favour. At seventeen Ernestine left home. She travelled to Berlin, where an anti-Semitic law that required all non-Prussian Jews to have a Prussian sponsor. She then travelled to Belgium, the Netherlands, France, and finally England.

In England, she met the Utopian socialist Robert Owen. She helped him to set up the Association of All Classes of All Nations, a group that campaigned for universal human rights and internationalism. She met William Ella Rose, an Owenite and they were married by a civil magistrate.

In May 1836 the Roses emigrated to New York where Ernestine began to give lectures advocating the abolition of slavery, free public education and equality for women. In the South, Ernestine was the target of threats and abuse. In 1855, a local newspaper in Maine called her 'a female Atheist... a thousand times below a prostitute.'

In 1869, she successfully lobbied in New York to allow married women to retain their own property and have equal guardianship of children. In 1869, she made the closing address at the nationwide Women's Rights Convention, but her health took a downward turn, and she and her husband set sail for England, seeking rest and recuperation.

By 1873 her health had improved enough for her to resume her campaigning for women's suffrage in England. She attended the Conference of the Woman's Suffrage Movement in London and spoke in Edinburgh at a large public meeting in favour of woman's suffrage. She died in Brighton, in 1892.

18 May
Sanité Bélair and the Haitian Revolution (1781-1802)

Sanité Belair was a female Haitian Freedom fighter and revolutionary and a lieutenant in the army of Toussaint Louverture. Sanité was born an Affranchi, a free person of colour, in Verrettes, Haiti, in 1781. This was the year that a revolt against French colonial rule broke out. This revolt became the Haitian Revolution, a successful insurrection by self-liberated slaves. Ex-slave Toussaint Louverture emerged as Haiti's most charismatic hero. Sanité married Charles Bélair in 1796 when she was fifteen years old. Charles was a Brigade commander and he later became a general in the revolutionary army. Sanité became a sergeant and later a lieutenant. During the revolutionary wars, the Belairs were pursued by a column of French soldiers led by Faustin Répussard. The couple took refuge in the Artibonite department but Répussard launched a surprise attack and captured Sanité. Her husband surrendered so that he would not be separated from Sanité. The Belairs were both sentenced to death by the French military. Charles was to be executed by firing squad and Sanité was to be decapitated. She was forced to watch Charles's execution and refused the blindfold as she was led to the execution block. She was twenty-one years old. The Haitian revolution ended in 1804 and the former colony won its independence. The Haitian Revolution was the only slave uprising that led to the creation of a state free from slavery and ruled by non-whites and former captives. Sanité's revolution is now widely seen as a defining moment in the history of the Atlantic World. Sanité Bélair is remembered as one of the heroes of the Haitian Revolution. In 2004, she was the only woman featured on banknotes designed for the 'Bicentennial of Haiti' Commemorative series.

20 May
Margarita Neri and the Mexican Revolution (1865-?)

M argarita Neri, 'The Rebel Queen of Morelos', was the daughter of a Mayan Indian and a former Mexican general who had rebelled against the repressive government of President Diaz around 1900.

The Mexican Revolution began on 20 November 1910 and raged well into the 1920s. The revolution was carried out by revolutionaries against dictator Porfirio Diaz Mori and to establish both democracy and reforms for the impoverished peasants.

The conflict was bloody, with around 900,000 people losing their lives. Despite facing persistent inequality and sexism, women insisted on playing a major role in the overthrow of the old regime.

The most famous of all the *soldaderas* was Margarita Neri, who not only fought as a soldier in the war but was also a commander. From 1910, Margarita commanded a force of over 1,000 rebels who swept through the Tabasco and Chiapas regions. Margarita was so effective in her slaughter of anti-revolutionary troops that when the Governor of Guerrero heard that she was approaching with her forces, he hid in a crate. Her soldiers represented a serious threat to the Mexican Government.

In 1911, the *Los Angeles Times* reported on revolutionary battles taking place in Guerrero, a southern state in Mexico. 'Petticoat leads band of Rebels,' the headline blared, in a story picked up right across North America, the paper reported, she was a daring raider.

Margarita developed a reputation as a brutal and fiery leader, and was known for her passionate dancing—and her threat to personally 'decapitate Diaz.' Margarita was reportedly executed, but the place and time of her death are unknown. We do know that the Mexican Revolution she fought for succeeded in transforming Mexican society.

21 May
So much more than Malcolm X's mum: Louise Little
(1897-1989)

Yesterday was Malcolm X's birthday, so today's post is about his mum.

Louise Little was born in Grenada, daughter of Edith Langdon. Edith was herself the daughter of Jupiter and Mary Jane Langdon. When she was eleven years old, Edith was raped by a Scottish man named Edward Norton and she later gave birth to a baby named Louise. Louise was raised by her grandparents and became fluent in English, French and Grenadian Creole French. After her grandmother's death in 1917, she emigrated to Montreal, where her uncle introduced her to the ideas of Marcus Garvey and the Universal Negro Improvement Association (UNIA). Through the UNIA, Louise met Earl Little and they married on 10 May, 1919. The following year the Littles moved to Philadelphia, and then to Omaha, Nebraska. While in Omaha, Louise was active in the UNIA's local chapter. Louise was pregnant with Malcolm when the Klan visited the family's house one night. They shouted threats and demanded that the Littles leave town because Earl was 'spreading trouble'. By 1926, Klan threats drove the family to move to Milwaukee and then to Lansing, Michigan. There the family was harassed by the Black Legion, a local white racist group. The family home was burned down in 1929 and in 1931 tragedy struck when Earl died in what was officially ruled a street-car accident. Louise always believed he had been murdered by the Black Legion.

In 1937, a pregnant Louise was abandoned by her lover and in late 1938 she was committed to Kala-mazoo State Hospital. The children were separated and sent to foster homes.

Louise was in hospital to 1963, well over twenty-five years. Her son Malcolm X joined his siblings in campaigning to secure her release. She lived with her surviving family for another thirty years.

22 May
The Poplar revolt and Minnie Lansbury (1889-1922)

Minnie on her
way to prison,
1921

M innie Glassman, the daughter of Jewish
coal merchant Isaac Glassman, was born in
Stepney in 1889. She became a schoolteacher
and an activist in the campaign for women's
suffrage. In 1913, Minnie and the radical labour
politicians George Lansbury and Kier Hardy,
supported Sylvia Pankhurst as she established
the East London Federation of Suffragettes (ELF)
to fight for socialism and demand for women's
suffrage. The ELF provided a socialist alternative
to the Women's Social and Political Union, run
along increasingly autocratic line by her mother
Emmeline and sister Christabel.
In 1914 Millie married Edgar Lansbury, the son of
George Lansbury, who was the Labour Party MP
for Bromley and Bow. Millie was a key figure in
the radical East End's opposition to World War I.
In 1918 Minnie was elected Assistant Secretary of
the Workers' Socialist Federation.
Siblings Edgar, Violet and Daisy Lansbury all
joined the Communist Party. Daisy was active
alongside Sylvia Pankhurst. Violet spent many

years in Russia and married Anglo-Indian communist Clemens Palme Dutt, older brother of Rajani Palme Dutt, a prominent British member of the Communist Party.

In November 1919, Minnie was elected to Poplar Council. The Labour Party had won a landslide of 39 seats out of the 42 council seats available. In 1921 George Lansbury proposed that the Council stop collecting the rates for cross-London bodies based outside Poplar. On 31 March, 1921, Poplar Council set a rate of 4s 4d instead of 6s 10d. On 29 April, the Councillors were summoned to court. They were told that they had to pay the rates or go to prison – they chose prison. At one meeting Millie said, 'Poplar will pay its share of London's rates when Westminster, Kensington, and the City do the same.'

On 28 August over 4,000 people demonstrated at Tower Hill in support of the councillors, but the councillors were arrested on 1 September. Five women Councillors, including Millie Lansbury, were sent to Holloway Prison. Twenty-five men, including George Lansbury, went to Brixton Prison. On 21 September, public pressure led the government to release Nellie Cressall, a councillor who was six months pregnant.

When several Metropolitan Borough Councils announced their attention to follow Poplar's example, the government was forced to back down. On 12 October, the councillors were set free but Minnie had developed pneumonia in prison and she died on 1 January, 1922 aged just 32. Her memorial clock can still be found on Bow Road. Actress Angela Lansbury is the daughter of Edgar Lansbury and his second wife. Angela is a Democrat supporter in America, supports the Labour party in Britain. 'How could I not?' she replied to an interviewer's question, 'I'm not an active member but many members of my family are very much involved.'

23 May
Rebel against British oppression: Nanny of the Maroons
(1686-1755)

Nanny was born into slavery sometime during the 1680s, on the Gold Coast, now Ghana. She escaped from a British colony in Jamaica and led a group of slaves into the inner mountain areas of the island. Soon large communities of ex-slaves, calling themselves Maroons, gathered around her. They founded an independent settlement called Nanny Town around 1723. From this town up in the mountains, Nanny was able to lead raids against plantations and liberate slaves. Her revolution quickly captured the attention of the British and a series of campaigns against the Maroons were launched.

Nanny and the Maroons were innovators in guerilla warfare. They used surprise, knowledge of the terrain, and cleverly chosen positions in their fight against the British. Their village was located in rugged territory and had only one possible entrance so attacking soldiers were easily ambushed by camouflaged troops. Nanny never killed all the members of any attacking force. She allowed one or two to return to tell the horror of the massacre.

Nanny Town itself was attacked on a number of occasions, in 1730, 1731, 1732, and one British attack in 1734 finally captured the settlement. Nanny and the survivors fled to set up another camp, from which they proved just as defiant.

Although Nanny and her people faced nearly constant attack and hunger, they remained united and strong against the British. From 1739-40, the British were forced to sign a peace treaty with the Maroons, giving them 500 acres of land to call their own.

Nanny, whose image is on the Jamaican $500 bill, remains a powerful symbol of the resistance to slavery.

24 May
Chartist, feminist, journalist and communist:
Helen MacFarlane (1818-1860)

Helen Macfarlane was born in Barrhead, Paisley, Scotland. Her father, George, owned a calico-printing works. There was radicalism in the Macfarlane family and amongst the mill workers who were solid supporters of Chartism. In 1842 the Macfarlane mills went bust and the family were utterly ruined. Helen had to take employment as a governess. By 1848 Helen was in Vienna when the Revolution against the Habsburg Monarchy broke out. She wrote: 'I am free to confess that, for me the most joyful of all spectacles possible; one which I enjoyed extremely at Vienna, in March 1848, a universal tumbling of impostors. For it amounts to this, that men are determined to live no longer in lies!' Following the defeat of the 1848 Revolution Helen returned to Britain, first to Burnley, then to London. She began to write for the paper of radical Chartist George Julian Harney, *The Red Republican*, and became friends with Karl Marx and Friedrich Engels.

Historians of philosophy have ignored Helen's role as the first British commentator on, and translator of, the writing of Hegel, whose works were important to the emerging British socialist movement. Helen saw Chartist tactics as less effective than the revolutionary French Blanquists: 'How comes it that our French brothers have done so much compared with us? Because they are organised into one compact mass, which, under the guidance of competent leaders, moves like an army of well-disciplined soldiers, steadily onward to a given point.'

In 1850 Austrian General Haynau, infamous butcher of the 1848 Revolution, visited London. Workers at the Barclay Perkins brewery tried to drown him in a vat of beer then chased him down the street. There was a press outcry, but

Helen wrote, 'Had I been present when those brave proletarians gave this ruffian his desserts, I should certainly have dissuaded the mob from... laying hands on him... brothers, your hands are blackened and hardened from honest toil. Do not pollute them from touching that beast. Take mops and brooms, sweep him out as you do other kinds of dirt. Like to like. Filth to filth. Haynau to the common sewer.'

Helen published the first translation of *The Communist Manifesto* in English in *The Red Republican* in 1850. When Helen fell out with Harney at the end of 1850, Marx commented that Harney had broken with, 'the only collaborator on his spouting rag who had original ideas – a rare bird, on his paper...'

In 1852 Helen married Francis Proust and in 1853 she gave birth to a daughter named Consuela Pauline Roland Proust (Pauline Roland was one of the most prominent female leaders of the 1848 Revolution). In 1853 the family sailed to a new life in South Africa, but Francis died on the journey and Consuela died days after arriving in South Africa.

Helen returned to England and in 1856 she married Reverend John Wilkinson Edwards who was a widower with eleven children. She gave birth to two boys, Herbert and Walter. Helen completely dropped out of public life and in 1860, at the age of 41, she fell ill with bronchitis and died.

Poem:
Walt Whitman: Resurgemus, written to celebrate the European
revolutions of 1848

SUDDENLY, out of its state and drowsy air, the air of slaves,
Like lightning Europe le'pt forth,
Sombre, superb and terrible,
As Ahimoth, brother of Death.
God, 'twas delicious!
That brief, tight, glorious grip
Upon the throats of kings.

You liars paid to defile the People,
Mark you now:
Not for numberless agonies, murders, lusts,
For court thieving in its manifold mean forms,
Worming from his simplicity the poor man's wages;
For many a promise sworn by royal lips
And broken, and laughed at in the breaking;
Then, in their power, not for all these,
Did a blow fall in personal revenge,
Or a hair draggle in blood:
The People scorned the ferocity of kings.

But the sweetness of mercy brewed bitter destruction,
And frightened rulers come back:
Each comes in state, with his train,
Hangman, priest, and tax-gatherer,
Soldier, lawyer, and sycophant;
An appalling procession of locusts,
And the king struts grandly again.

Yet behind all, lo, a Shape
Vague as the night, draped interminably,

Head, front and form, in scarlet folds;
Whose face and eyes none may see,
Out of its robes only this,
The red robes, lifted by the arm,
One finger pointed high over the top,
Like the head of a snake appears.

Meanwhile, corspes lie in new-made graves,
Bloody corpses of young men;
The rope of the gibbet hangs heavily,
The bullets of tyrants are flying,
The creatures of power laugh aloud:
And all these things bear fruits, and they are good.

Those corpses of young men,
Those martyrs that hang from the gibbets,
Those hearts pierced by the grey lead,
Cold and motionless as they seem,
Live elsewhere with undying vitality;
They live in other young men, O, kings,
They live in brothers, again ready to defy you;
They were purified by death,
They were taught and exalted.

Not a grave of those slaughtered ones,
But is growing its seed of freedom,
In its turn to bear seed,
Which the winds shall carry afar and resow,
And the rain nourish.

Not a disembodied spirit
Can the weapon of tyrants let loose,
But it shall stalk invisibly over the earth,
Whispering, counseling, cautioning.
Liberty, let others despair of thee,
But I will never despair of thee:
Is the house shut? Is the master away?
Nevertheless, be ready, be not weary of watching,
He will surely return; his messengers come anon.

25 May Many thanks to Andy Daglish and Ana Daglish de Almeida for introducing today's re-bellious daughter the **Portuguese Anti-fascist icon Catarina Eufémia** (1928-1954)

This month marks the anniversary of the assassination of Catarina Eufémia, a young militant agricultural worker who was gunned down for answering back to a police officer whilst canvassing support for a strike in Alentejo on 19 May, 1954. Catarina became an icon for resistance against the fascist government of Salazar.

Catarina was born in Baleizão in the most arid and hot region of Portugal into a family of jornaleiros (daylabourers). By the age of seventeen she was married and had been working in the fields for years. By 1954 she was the mother of three children and was pregnant with a fourth.

In 1954 agricultural workers demanded an increase in pay from 16 escudos to 23, still a pitiful amount. The landowners not only refused to pay but also hired other labour from different parts of the region.

On hearing that other agricultural labourers had been hired, Catarina and fourteen women workers went to address them as they arrived and appealed for solidarity. However, the police had arrived before them. Undeterred, Catarina approached the workers but was stopped by a GNR (national police) agent who asked her what she wanted. 'Only bread and work', she replied. The agent, considering her reply to be impudent gunned her down with a machine gun. She died minutes later and the eight-month-old child she was carrying in her arms was injured. The agent was never prosecuted.

The police attacked Catarina's funeral and some mourners were sentenced to two years jail on trumped up charges. Catarina became a symbol of struggle throughout Portugal, she was an emblem of growing resistance to the Salazarista regime but it would be twenty years before her hopes would flourish in the Portuguese Revolution of 1974.

26 May
The pioneering black communist: Grace Campbell (1883-1943)

G race Campbell was born in 1882 in Georgia. Her father was a Jamaican immigrant and a teacher and her mother was a woman of mixed African American and Native American heritage. The family moved to New York City in 1905 and Grace devoted herself to community projects such as the Empire Friendly Shelter, a home for unmarried mothers.

In 1911, she became the first black woman to be appointed as a parole officer in the Court of General Sessions for the City of New York. She worked as a jail attendant in the women's section at 'the Tombs', New York's infamous prison, until her death in 1943.

Grace became active in the Socialist Party of America and was probably the first African American woman to join the party. Her involvement in the Socialist Party in New York placed her in a community of radical women, many of whom were gay and bi-sexual. The women campaigned for birth control, free love and gender equality.

In 1920, Grace helped found the People's Educational Forum in 1920, a forum for debating socialist and black nationalist ideas.

Grace played a pioneering role in Harlem's early 20th century radicalism and was the most prominent woman in the Harlem Left.

In 1919 and 1920, Grace ran for office in the New York State Assembly on the Socialist ticket. Her groundbreaking ticket won 10% of the vote, nearly 2,000 votes, more than any other black Socialist party candidate. Grace was the first African-American woman to run for public office in the state of New York.

In 1921, she moved away from the Socialist party and was a founding members of the African Blood Brotherhood, which advocated armed self-defence, equal rights, and self-determination and was known as the first black communist organisation. Grace was the only woman in the leadership of the organisation, which met in her Harlem apartment. Her home remained a busy hub of radical political activity into the 1930s. In 1923, Grace became the first black woman to join the Communist Workers' Party and she soon worked as a party organiser. She combined community work with a socialist political vision. At the centre of Grace's politics was the aspiration for world revolution, concern for black women's freedom and a passionate commitment to the communist movement. In later years, Grace fell out with the Stalinist leadership of the international communist movement.

Grace was monitored by the FBI, which noted that she carried the Bolshevik red card and reported that, 'Grace Campbell showed herself an ardent Communist . . . Though employed by the City Administration, is frank in her disapproval of it and said the only way to remedy the present situation was to install Bolshevism in place of the present Government' (FBI, 4 March, 1931).

Grace never married or had children. She continued her work in socialist politics and the prison service until her death in 1943, aged 60.

Grace Campbell addressing a Harlem rally

27 May
Not just Mrs Lenin: Nadezhda Krupskaya (1869-1939)

Nadezhda (Nadya) Krupskaya was born to a noble but impoverished Russian family. She won a medal at school but was excluded from higher education because she was a woman. Nadya was already a well-read Marxist and a teacher familiar with working-class life in St Petersburg when she met Vladimir Lenin in 1894. In October 1896 she was arrested and was allowed to join Lenin in exile in Siberia on condition that they married.

In 1900 Nadya published a pamphlet, *The Woman Worker*, which explained how working women could liberate themselves as part of the working-class movement. Released from exile in 1901, Krupskaya joined Lenin and spent five years in Munich, Paris and London. Leon Trotsky described how Nadya, 'received comrades when they arrived, instructed them when they left, established connections, supplied secret addresses, wrote letters, and coded and decoded correspondence. In her room there was always a smell of burned paper from the secret letters she heated over the fire to read'.

After the 1905 Revolution, Nadya returned to St Petersburg and became secretary of the Central Committee before being forced back into exile. She was one of the first Marxists to formulate a socialist theory of education. She wrote *Public Education and Democracy,* which was published following the revolution of 1917.

Revolution toppled the Tsar in February 1917 and the exiles returned to Russia. In the summer of 1917, Nadya became a member of the Vyborg Bolshevik Committee. She was also chair of the Vyborg Committee for Relief of Soldier's Wives. Vyborg was a large working-class district of the renamed Petrograd and winning support there was crucial for the socialist project.

In August 1917, Krupskaya was a delegate to the Sixth Party Congress in Petrograd. On 5 October she was one of a seven-person delegation from the Vyborg District to the Bolshevik Central Committee argued in favour of the October Revolution. Following the success of the October Revolution, Nadya joined a government body devoted to eradicating illiteracy and setting up libraries. She became a prolific author and orator. Her bi-ographer wrote that she, 'hurled herself at a furious pace into the impossible task of designing and constructing a human, cultivated socialist system of education in a country that was economically ruined, racked by civil war'.

Free and universal access to education was mandated for all children and the number of schools doubled within the first two years of the revolution. Co-education was immediately implemented to combat sex discrimination, and for the first time, schools were created for pupils with disabilities.

Nadya survived for fifteen years after Lenin's death in 1924, both defending Lenin's legacy and making compromises with Stalin in order to survive. She dedicated her life to the struggle for a better world and must be considered as a revolutionary in her own right.

Nadezhda Krupskaya: Giving a propaganda speech in 1920 during the civil war.

(© RGASPI Moscow)

28 May
Chartist militant and theoretician: Elizabeth Hanson
(1797-1886)

lizabeth was born in 1797. She married Abram
Hanson, a shoemaker, and lived near Halifax.
Elizabeth became politically active in the
campaign against the Poor Law Amendment
Act of 1834. The act stated that the destitute
would only get help if they entered a workhouse,
where families were forced apart and prison-like
regimes were enforced.

Elizabeth was furious that the legislation 'cast
women in the role of dependants on their
husbands' incomes rather than as contributors to
the family income on their own right'. In February
1838, Elizabeth told a meeting that women in
the workhouse had their hair cropped and were
separated from their children. She argued that the
only way to stop this was for women to unite and
form political organisations.

Elizabeth Hanson and Mary Grassby formed the
Elland Female Radical Association in March,
1838. The Association supported the campaign
for the Charter. She became one of the movement's most effective speakers, and a newspaper
reported she 'melted the hearts and drew forth
floods of tears'.

Like all radical women, Elizabeth and Mary
were attacked and ridiculed in the national press
– working-class women were not supposed to
interfere in politics.

In 1839 Elizabeth gave birth to a son, who she
named Feargus O'Connor, after the Chartist
leader. She continued to be involved in the campaign for universal suffrage. Elizabeth's husband
Abram recognised 'the women who are the best
politicians, the best revolutionists, and the best
political economists.'

Poem:
Carl Sandburg: I Am the People, the Mob

I Am the People, the Mob
I am the people—the mob—the crowd—the mass.
Do you know that all the great work of the world is done through me?
I am the workingman, the inventor, the maker of the world's food
    and clothes.
I am the audience that witnesses history. The Napoleons come from
    me and the Lincolns. They die. And then I send forth more
    Napoleons and Lincolns.
I am the seed ground. I am a prairie that will stand for much plowing.
Terrible storms pass over me. I forget. The best of me is sucked out
    and wasted.
I forget. Everything but Death comes to me and makes me work and
    give up what I have. And I forget.
Sometimes I growl, shake myself and spatter a few red drops for
    history to remember. Then—I forget.
When I, the People, learn to remember, when I, the People, use the
    lessons of yesterday and no longer forget who robbed me last year,
    who played me for a fool—then there will be no speaker in all the
    world say the name:
'The People,' with any fleck of a sneer in his voice or any far-off smile
    of derision.
The mob—the crowd—the mass—will arrive then'.

29 May
Communard: Louise Michel (1830-1905)

Louise Michel was born in 1830, the illegitimate daughter of a serving-maid. She was raised by her grandparents. In 1865 Louise opened a progressive school in Paris and became involved in the radical politics. In 1869 Louise joined a feminist group, the Society for the Demand of Civil Rights for Women.

When Paris came under siege from Prussian troops in 1870, Louise joined the National Guard. The French government tried to disarm the National Guard and the city rose up in protest. The Paris Commune was declared in 1871 and Louise was elected head of the Montmartre Women's Vigilance Committee.

Louise played a leading role in the revolutionary government of the Paris Commune and the armed struggle against the French government. She fought with the 61st Battalion of Montmartre and organised ambulance stations. In her memoirs she recalled, 'I like the smell of gunpowder, grapeshot flying through the air, but above all, I'm devoted to the Revolution.' She also challenged her male comrades to 'play a part in the struggle for women's rights, after men and women have won the rights of all humanity?'

The Commune was brutally suppressed and around 20,000 men, women and children were executed. In December 1871, Louise was charged with trying to overthrow the government, encouraging citizens to arm themselves and using weapons. Defiantly, she dared the judges to sentence her to death. She was sentenced to penal transportation, one of some 10,000 Communards who were deported. After twenty months in prison, Michel was deported to New Caledonia, where she met Nathalie Lemel, another female Communard. Louise taught French to the local Kanak people and took their side in the 1878 Kanak revolt. She became a teacher for the children of deported Communards.

In 1880, amnesty was granted to Communards and Louise returned to Paris where she con-tin-ued her revolutionary activity. She attended the anarchist congress in London in 1881, where she addressed huge crowds.

In Paris in March 1883 Louise led a demonstra-tion by unemployed workers which ended in riot. She was tried for her actions and used the court to publicly defend her principles. She was sentenced to six years of solitary confinement.

In 1890 she was arrested again and escaped to London where she set up a progressive school for refugee children.

Louise returned to France in 1895. She died of pneumonia in Marseille on 10 January, 1905. Her funeral in Paris was attended by more than 100,000 people.

■ Louise Michel wrote this poem in memory of her great friend, the Communard Théophile Ferré, who refused to recognize a military court's right to judge him after the defeat of the Com-mune, and was sentenced to death and executed.

Red Carnations

If one day to the cold cemetery I were to go,
brothers, cast on your sister,
like a final hope,
some red carnations in bloom.
In the final days of the empire,
as the people awoke,
red carnation, it was your smile
that told us all was reborn.
And now, go blossom in the shade
of dark and drear prisons,
go blossom near the somber captive,
and tell him we love him.
Tell him that in these changing times
everything belongs to the future;
that the victor with his pallid brow
can die as easily as the vanquished.

30 May: Guest post from the great writer Jack Robertson
Red Clydeside Rent Strike leader: Mary Barbour (1875-1958

Mary Barbour was born in the Renfrewshire
village of Kilbarchan in 1875, daughter and
third child of seven to James Rough, a carpet
weaver, and his wife, Jane Gavin. Mary left school
at the age of fourteen and went to work as a
thread twister and then carpet printer. After her
marriage to engineering worker, David Barbour,
the couple settled in Govan where she became an
active member of the Kinning Park Co-Operative
Guild, the first to be established in Scotland. She
joined the Independent Labour Party and took
part in the Socialist Sunday School.
By the outbreak of the First World War,
Glasgow was a centre of the munitions industry.
Discontent grew among the workers and led
to widespread strike action in the engineering
industry, much of it involving women and
unskilled labour. The trigger for what became
known as Red Clydeside was a strike of women
workers at the Singer sewing machines factory in
Clydebank, when the workforce of 11,000 came
out in solidarity with twelve female colleagues in
March 1911.
Housing conditions is Glasgow at the time were
appalling. Writing about what he called Glasgow's
Housing Disgrace, one of the leaders of the First
Shop Stewards' Movement on Clydeside, Harry
McShane, wrote that 'thousands of families are
denied a decent home life...in some houses, three,
four an five persons share the same bed...the
houses in which they live are rat infested.'
When Glasgow landlords, or factors, tried to
impose huge rent increases at the same time as
young men of fighting age were being sent to
fight in France, Mary Barbour was instrumental
in forming the South Govan Women's Housing
Association. She was then a working-class
housewife with two sons and her husband was

employed in the shipyards. The Govan organising committee prevented evictions, blocking the entrance to tenement blocks and the hounding of Sherriff's Officers.

In his memoir, *Revolt on the Clyde*, the Clydeside MP, Willie Gallagher wrote: 'Street meetings, back-court meetings, drums, bells, trumpets – every method was used to bring the women out and organise them for the struggle. Notices were printed by the thousand and put up in windows: wherever you went you could see them. In street after street, scarcely a window without one: We Are Not Paying Increased Rent'.

Rent strikes soon spread to the entire Clydeside area and culminated, in November 1915, with one of the biggest demonstrations in Glasgow's political history: thousands of women and thousands of shipyard and engineering workers paraded to the Sherriff's Court 'where the demonstration was near riot proportions'. The protestors became known as 'Mary Barbour's Army' and included other leading women fighters such as Agnes Dollan, Helen Crawfurd, Mary Laird and Mary Jeff.

Mary Barbour became a founding member of the Women's Peace Crusade, which campaigned for a negotiated settlement to World War I. Later she stood as a Labour candidate for the Fairfield ward in Govan and became one of the first women councillors elected to Glasgow Town Council. In March 2018, after a long battle, a statue commemorating Mary Barbour was unveiled at Govan Cross in Glasgow. Her image also forms part of the commemorative mural displayed on the west side of the Clutha Bar, the site of a helicopter crash in 2013.

Poem: Continuing the Scottish theme set by Jack Robertson:
Robert Burns: The Rights of Woman (1792)

While Europe's eye is fix'd on mighty things,
The fate of Empires and the fall of Kings;
While quacks of State must each produce his plan,
And even children lisp the Rights of Man;
Amid this mighty fuss just let me mention,
The Rights of Woman merit some attention.

First, in the Sexes' intermix'd connection,
One sacred Right of Woman is, protection.
The tender flower that lifts its head, elate,
Helpless, must fall before the blasts of Fate,
Sunk on the earth, defac'd its lovely form,
Unless your shelter ward th' impending storm.

Our second Right – but needless here is caution,
To keep that right inviolate's the fashion;
Each man of sense has it so full before him,
He'd die before he'd wrong it – 'tis decorum.
There was, indeed, in far less polish'd days,
A time, when rough rude man had naughty ways,
Would swagger, swear, get drunk, kick up a riot,
Nay even thus invade a Lady's quiet.

Now, thank our stars! those Gothic times are fled;
Now, well-bred men – and you are all well-bred –
Most justly think (and we are much the gainers)
Such conduct neither spirit, wit, nor manners.

For Right the third, our last, our best, our dearest,
That right to fluttering female hearts the nearest;
Which even the Rights of Kings, in low prostration,
Most humbly own – 'tis dear, dear admiration!
In that blest sphere alone we live and move;
There taste that life of life-immortal love.
Smiles, glances, sighs, tears, fits , flirtations, airs ;
'Gainst such an host what flinty savage dares,
When awful Beauty joins with all her charms
Who is so rash as rise in rebel arms?

But truce with kings, and truce with constitutions,
With bloody armaments and revolutions;
Let Majesty your first attention summon,
Ah! ca ira! The Majesty Of Woman!

31 May Only one choice possible today:
Black revolutionary Angela Davis (1944-)

Angela was born in Birmingham, Alabama, in the 'Dynamite Hill' area, where houses were bombed to drive out middle-class black families. Her mother, Sallye Bell Davis, was an organizer of the Southern Negro Youth Congress, which was influenced by the Communist Party.

As a Girl Scout, Angela marched and picketed to protest racial segregation in Birmingham and joined a communist youth movement. She studied French at Brandeis University and she was in Biarritz when she learned of the 1963 Birmingham church bombing by the Ku Klux Klan, in which four black girls were killed.

Angela studied philosophy at the University of Frankfurt in under the Marxist philosopher Herbert Marcuse, later recalling that he, 'taught me that it was possible to be an academic, an activist, a scholar, and a revolutionary'.

Back in the US, Angela studied at the University of California before moving to East Germany, where she gained a doctorate at the Humboldt University of Berlin.

Returning again to the US, she joined the Communist Party and was active in the women's movement, the Black Panther Party, and the campaign against the Vietnam War. In 1969, she told a meeting: 'We are facing a common enemy and that enemy is Yankee Imperialism, which is killing us both here and abroad. Now I think anyone who would try to separate those struggles, anyone who would say that in order to consolidate an anti-war movement, we have to leave all of these other outlying issues out of the picture, is playing right into the hands of the enemy.'

In 1969 she was fired as acting assistant professor of philosophy at the University of California (UCLA) because of her Communist Party membership. A court ruled her dismissal illegal, so the university fired her again this time for using inflammatory language.

Davis supported the Soledad Brothers, three inmates who were accused of killing a prison guard at Soledad Prison. In 1970, firearms registered to Davis were used in an armed takeover of a courtroom in California. The teenage brother of a Soledad prisoner, George Jackson, led the raid but when police starting shooting, four people, including the judge, were killed.

A warrant was issued for Angela's arrest. The FBI director J Edgar Hoover listed Davis on the FBI's Ten Most Wanted Fugitive List. When she was finally captured, President Richard M. Nixon congratulated the FBI on its 'capture of the dangerous terrorist Angela Davis'. Thousands of people began organising a movement to win her release. John Lennon and Yoko Ono contributed to this campaign with the song 'Angela'.

On 4 June, 1972, an all-white jury returned a verdict of not guilty. After her acquittal, Davis went on an international speaking tour which included Cuba, where she had previously been received by Fidel Castro in 1969 as a member of a Communist Party delegation.

In the 1980s she was professor of ethnic studies at San Francisco State University. Much of her work focused on the abolition of prisons. In 1991, Angela left the CP and joined the Committees of Correspondence for Democracy and Socialism. Angela joined the feminist studies department at the University of California, Santa Cruz. She has received various awards, including the Lenin Peace Prize. In 2001 Angela spoke out against the war on terror following the 9/11 attacks. She supports the Boycott, Divestment and Sanctions campaign against Israel.

In 2017 Angela was an honorary co-chair of the Women's March on Washington, in protest of President Trump's inauguration. Most recently, she has been a prominent supporter of the Black Lives Matter protests.

Song:
Nina Simone: Mississippi Goddam

The name of this tune is Mississippi Goddam
And I mean every word of it

Alabama's gotten me so upset
Tennessee made me lose my rest
And everybody knows about Mississippi Goddam

Alabama's gotten me so upset
Tennessee made me lose my rest
And everybody knows about Mississippi Goddam

Can't you see it
Can't you feel it
It's all in the air
I can't stand the pressure much longer
Somebody say a prayer

Alabama's gotten me so upset
Tennessee made me lose my rest
And everybody knows about Mississippi Goddam

This is a show tune
But the show hasn't been written for it, yet

Hound dogs on my trail
School children sitting in jail
Black cat cross my path
I think every day's gonna be my last

Lord have mercy on this land of mine
We all gonna get it in due time
I don't belong here
I don't belong there
I've even stopped believing in prayer

Don't tell me
I tell you
Me and my people just about due
I've been there so I know
They keep on saying "Go slow!"

But that's just the trouble
"do it slow"

Washing the windows
"do it slow"
Picking the cotton
"do it slow"
You're just plain rotten
"do it slow"
You're too damn lazy
"do it slow"
The thinking's crazy
"do it slow"
Where am I going
What am I doing
I don't know
I don't know

Just try to do your very best
Stand up be counted with all the rest
For everybody knows about Mississippi Goddam

I made you thought I was kiddin'

Picket lines
School boy cots
They try to say it's a communist plot
All I want is equality
for my sister my brother my people and me

Yes you lied to me all these years
You told me to wash and clean my ears
And talk real fine just like a lady
And you'd stop calling me Sister Sadie

Oh but this whole country is full of lies
You're all gonna die and die like flies
I don't trust you any more
You keep on saying "Go slow!"
"Go slow!"

But that's just the trouble
"do it slow"
Desegregation
"do it slow"

Mass participation
"do it slow"
Reunification
"do it slow"
Do things gradually
"do it slow"
But bring more tragedy
"do it slow"
Why don't you see it
Why don't you feel it
I don't know
I don't know

You don't have to live next to me
Just give me my equality
Everybody knows about Mississippi
Everybody knows about Alabama
Everybody knows about Mississippi Goddam

That's it!

Freedom Riders, 1964 activists sing before leaving training sessions at Western College for Women in Oxford, Ohio, for Mississippi in June 1964.

1 June
America Rising: Fannie Lou Hamer (1917–1977)

"We been waitin' all our lives, and still gettin'
killed, still gettin' hung, still gettin' beat to death.
Now we're tired waitin'!" —Fannie Lou Hamer

Fannie Lou Townsend was born in Montgomery
County, Mississippi, the youngest of twenty
children. The family's animals were poisoned
by a local white supremacist so in 1919 the
Townsend family moved to Sunflower County,
Mississippi where they worked as sharecroppers.
From the age of six Fanny Lou picked cotton with
her family, able to go to school only in winter.
At the age of twelve she left school completely to
support her aging parents.
In 1945, Fanny Lou married Perry 'Pap' Hamer,
a tractor driver. She wanted children but she had
been sterilized without her consent during stomach
surgery. Sterilisation was a weapon the state used
against African-American women in Mississippi.
The Hamers adopted two girls but one later died
after being denied admission to hospital because of
her mother's activism.
In 1962, Fanny Lou began her activism in the civil
rights movement. On August 31, she travelled with
other activists to Indianola, Mississippi, to register
to vote. She failed the complicated test and her
boss went ballistic when he found out what she had
done. 'I didn't try to register for you,' Hamer told
him, 'I tried to register for myself.' She was fired
and kicked off the plantation.
On 10 September, 1962, Fanny Lou was shot at sixteen times in a drive-by shooting by white suprem-
acists in retaliation for her attempt to vote. She
recalled 'I guess if I'd had any sense, I'd have been
a little scared — but what was the point of being
scared? The only thing they could do was kill me,
and it kinda seemed like they'd been trying to do
that a little bit at a time since I could remember'.

Fanny Lou finally passed the voter registration test on 10 January, 1963. She was active in the Student Nonviolent Coordinating Committee, registering others to vote. She was on a bus with activists in Winona, Mississippi when some activists went to local cafe where they were refused service. A highway patrolman arrested the whole group. Fanny Lou left the bus to find out what was happening and she was arrested too. Once in jail, Fanny Lou was brutally beaten and sexually assaulted. She suffered permanent kidney damage as a result of the assault. When she was released in 12 June, 1963 Fanny Lou returned to Mississippi to organise more voter registration drives.

She helped young volunteers including Sammy Younge Jr who was murdered in 1966 at a petrol station in Alabama, when he used a 'whites-only' restroom. In 1964, Fanny Lou helped co-found the Mississippi Freedom Democratic Party (MFDP), to challenge the racism of the Democratic Party. She unsuccessfully ran for a seat in the Senate.

Fanny Lou worked with Martin Luther King, Jr.'s Poor People's Campaign and published her autobiography in 1967. She began campaigning for poor sharecroppers. She pioneered the Freedom Farm Cooperative (FFC) in 1969 and established a food program called The Pig Project to provide food for impoverished sharecroppers' families.

Fanny Lou spent weeks in hospital for nervous exhaustion in January 1972, and was hospital-ised in January 1974 with a nervous breakdown. Two years later she was diagnosed with breast cancer and she died on 14 March, 1977, aged 59. Her tombstone is engraved with one of her famous quotes: 'I am sick and tired of being sick and tired.'

2 June
America Rising: Billie Holiday (1915-1959)

Billie Holiday was born Eleanora Fagan, on 7 April, 1915, in Philadelphia, the daughter of unmarried Sadie Fagan and Clarence Holiday, who left the family soon after her birth.
In 1925, when Billie was nine years old, she was brought before the juvenile court for truancy and sent to a Catholic reform school. She dropped out of school at the age of eleven. In 1926, a neighbour tried to rape Billie and she was taken protective custody as a state witness. Billie was released in February 1927, when she was nearly twelve, and she found a job running errands in a brothel.
By early 1929, Billie had joined her mother in Harlem where she became a prostitute.
Their house was raided on 2 May, 1929, and Holiday and her mother were sent to prison.
As a teenager, Billie started singing in nightclubs in Harlem. She made her first record at the age of eighteen in November 1933.
In the 1930s Billie's reputation as an exceptional jazz singer grew. She was one of the first black women to work with a white orchestra and toured in the segregated south where she was the target of racist abuse.
In November 1938, Billie was told to use the service lift at the Lincoln Hotel, instead of the

passenger lift. She recalled, 'I was never allowed to visit the bar or the dining room as did other members of the band ... [and] I was made to leave and enter through the kitchen.'

In 1938, Billie was introduced to 'Strange Fruit', a song based on a poem about lynching written by Abel Meeropol, a Jewish communist. The song reminded Billie of a father who died when he was denied medical treatment because of racism. It also spoke to generations of black people enraged by unceasing racist violence.

In September 1946, Holiday began work on her only major film, *New Orleans*, in which she starred opposite Louis Armstrong. Plagued by racism and McCarthyism, producer Jules Levey and script writer Herbert Biberman were pressed to avoid the impression that black people created jazz. In 1947 Biberman was listed as one of the Hollywood Ten and sent to jail.

By 1947, Billie was at the peak of her popularity and commercial success, but she was also consistently persecuted for her addiction to heroin. On 16 May, 1947, she was arrested for possession of narcotics in her New York apartment and sentenced to Alderson Federal Prison in Virginia. Billie was released on 16 March, 1948 and on 27 March she played Carnegie Hall to a sell out crowd. After the third curtain call, she passed out. Billie was arrested again on 22 January, 1949 in her room at the Hotel Mark Twain, San Francisco.

Billie's drug abuse, drinking, and relationships with abusive men caused her health to deteriorate. In July 1959, she was diagnosed with cirrhosis and was taken to Metropolitan Hospital in New York. The Federal Bureau of Narcotics were relentless in their targeting of Billie. She was again arrested and handcuffed for drug possession as she lay dying, her hospital room was raided, and she was placed under police guard. The guard was removed few hours before she died aged just 44.

3 June
America Rising: Joan Tarika Lewis (1950–)

Tarika grew up in the 1960s and studied at Oakland Tech, following in the steps of other Black Panther Party members Bobby Hutton and Reginald Forte. She was a talented violinist and jazz musician who became involved in racial politics at high school, where she co-founded the Black Student Union and staged sit-ins to demand the implementation of a Black Studies.
Tarika met founding members of the Black Panther Party, Bobby Seale and Huey Newton, and was inspired by their vision. She supported the Black Panther party's Community Survival Programs, like the Free Breakfast for Children, and Child Development Center.
In the spring of 1967, when she was sixteen, Lewis was one of the first women to formally join the Black Panther Party. She rose up through the ranks of the party, completing political education classes and training in handling weapons.
Tarika also supported the Black Panther Party through her work as a revolutionary graphic artist. She contributed over 40 images to the Black Panther newspaper between 1967 and 1969 under the pen name *Matilaba*. Her drawings showed armed Black Panther women, which was a shift from the very masculine representation of militant self-defence usually pictured.
Tarika left the Black Panther Party in January 1969 to devote herself to working as a graphic artist and Jazz violinist but she continued to support their campaigns. Tarika toured with saxophonist John Handy and went on to teach visual arts and jazz to inner city youth. She also is the founder of the Oakland Black String Ensemble.
Tarika published *Panther: A Pictorial History of the Black Panthers* and she worked as consultant on the 1995 Mario Van Peebles film *Panther* in which she had minor acting role.

6 June
America Rising: Leader of the Black Panthers: Elaine Brown
(1943-)

Elaine Brown grew up in inner city of North Philadelphia with her single mother Dorothy Clark. Despite desperate poverty, Dorothy worked hard to provide Elaine with a good education. Elaine moved to California and worked as a cocktail waitress at a strip club. She soon became involved with the Black Liberation Movement and began working for the radical newspaper *Harambee*.

Elaine became representative of the Black Student Alliance to the Black Congress of California. In April 1968, after the assassination of Martin Luther King Jr, Elaine joined the Los Angeles chapter of the Black Panther Party. She sold the Black Panther Party newspapers and learnt how to clean guns. Elaine helped the party to set up its first Free Breakfast for Children Program in Los Angeles and was central to the party's Free Busing to Prisons Program and Free Legal Aid Program. She became editor of the *Black Panther* publication issued by the Southern California Branch. Elaine also recorded two successful and deeply political albums, *Seize the Time* (Vault, 1969) and *Until We're Free* (Motown Records, 1973). In 1971, Elaine became a member of the Party's Central Committee as Minister of Education.

When Huey Newton fled to Cuba in 1974, he appointed Elaine to lead the Party, the only woman to do so. Elaine Brown chaired the Black Panther Party from 1974 until 1977. In her memoir she recalled gathering the Panthers together and telling them: 'I HAVE ALL THE GUNS AND ALL THE MONEY. I can withstand challenge from without and from within. Am I right, Comrade?... I'm telling you this because it's possible some of you may balk at a woman as the leader of the Black Panther Party. If this is your attitude, you'd

better get out of the Black Panther Party. Now...
If you are such an individual, you'd better run –
and fast! I am, as your chairman, the leader of this
party as of this moment. My leadership cannot be
challenged. I will lead our party both aboveground
and underground. I will lead the party not only in
furthering our goals but also in defending the party
by any and all means. They understood'.

In 1977, Elaine ran Lionel Wilson's victorious
campaign to become Oakland's first black mayor.
Elaine also developed the Panther's Liberation
School. Later that year, she left Oakland with
her daughter, Ericka, and moved to Los Angeles.
After leaving the Black Panther Party to raise her
daughter, Elaine worked on her powerful memoir,
A Taste of Power.

Elaine returned to the struggle for black liberation and was committed to radical prison reform.
From 1980 to 1983, she attended Southwestern
University School of Law in Los Angeles. In 1996,
Brown moved to Atlanta, Georgia, and founded
Fields of Flowers, Inc., a non-profit organisation
providing educational opportunities for impoverished African-American children. In 1998, she
founded the Michael Lewis Legal
Defense Committee, named after
a fourteen-year-old who was
sentenced to life in prison for a
murder he did not commit.

In 2003, Brown co-founded the
National Alliance for Radical
Prison Reform to campaign for
prison reform. From 1995 to the
present, she has lectured at more
than 40 colleges and universities,
as well as numerous conferences.

Panther women

In 2010, inmates in more than seven Georgia
prisons used contraband mobile phones to organize a nonviolent strike for better prison conditions, Brown became their 'closest adviser outside
prison walls'.

7 June
America Rising: From *Freedom Now* to *Black Power*: Kathleen Neal Cleaver (1945-)

Kathleen Neal Cleaver was born in Dallas, Texas. Her parents were both activists and college graduates of the University of Michigan. When her father joined the Foreign Service, the family travelled around the world but returned to the US after her brother died from leukaemia.

Kathleen continued to study until 1966, when she began working for the New York office of the Student Nonviolent Coordinating Committee (SNCC) after her childhood friend, Sammy Younge,* was murdered by racists.

Kathleen organised a conference at Fisk University in Nashville, Tennessee where she met Eldridge Cleaver, Minister of Information for the Black Panther Party. Kathleen moved to San Francisco in 1967 to join the Black Panther Party, and she married Eldridge. She became the Communications Secretary for the Panthers and organised demonstrations and press conferences, designed posters, and spoke at rallies and on TV. She was a central figure in the national campaign to free Huey Newton.

In 1968, the Cleavers' apartment was raided by the San Francisco Tactical Squad. Later that year, Eldridge was involved in a shoot out with Oakland police officers. He and two police officers were injured and Panther Bobby Hutton was killed. Eldridge was charged with attempted murder but he jumped bail and fled to Cuba and later to Algeria.

Kathleen was reunited with Eldridge in Algeria in 1969, where she gave birth to their two children. In 1971 the Cleavers formed a new organization called the Revolutionary People's Communication Network, which Kathleen returned to New York to promote..

In 1974, the French government granted legal

residency to the Cleavers, and the family was
reunited. A year later, the Cleavers moved back
to the US, and Eldridge was tried for the shootout in 1968 and found guilty of assault. Kathleen
worked on the Eldridge Cleaver Defense Fund
and he was freed on bail in 1976.
In later years, Eldridge moved to the right
politically. Kathleen left him and in 1981 she went
back to university. In 1987, she divorced Eldridge
and trained as a lawyer.
In 2005, she was Senior Research Associate at
the Yale Law School, and a Senior Lecturer in
the African American Studies department at Yale
University. She is currently serving as senior
lecturer at Emory University School of Law.
Kathleen has never stopped campaigning, for
example, for freedom for death-row inmate
Mumia Abu-Jamal. She has contributed to books
on feminism and racism and she helped to edit
El-dridge Cleaver' writings. She and other former
Black Panthers continue to meet.

*Sammy Younge is also mentioned in the section on Fanny Lou Hamer, p135.

Poem:
Brian Bilston: As I grow old I will march not shuffle

As I grow old
I will not shuffle to the beat
of self-interest
and make that slow retreat
to the right.

I will be a septuagenarian insurrectionist
marching with the kids. I shall sing
'La Marseillaise', whilst brandishing
homemade placards that proclaim
'DOWN WITH THIS SORT OF THING'.

I will be an octogenarian obstructionist,
and build unscalable barricades
from bottles of flat lemonade,
tartan blankets and chicken wire.
I will hurl prejudice upon the brazier's fire.

I will be a nonagenarian nonconformist,
armed with a ballpoint pen
and a hand that shakes with rage not age
at politicians' latest crimes,
in strongly-worded letters to The Times.

I will be a centenarian centurion
and allow injustice no admittance.
I will stage longstanding sit-ins.
My mobility scooter and I
will move for no-one.

And when I die
I will be the scattered ashes
that attach themselves to the lashes
and blind the eyes
of racists and fascists.

8 June: Today's post was written by Newham activist Shona Pollock:
Black Britain rising: Beryl Gilroy (1924-2001)

Beryl is an elusive character not least because claims that she was Britain's first black head-teacher have now been narrowed down to a man, but she was prodigious and assiduous in her devotion to Black literature and education.

Born Beryl Agatha Answick in 1924, she appears to have been the archetype of a British Guyanese woman, with a heady mix of bloods, as was common in Skeldon, a small port on the border with Dutch Guyana or Suriname.

She appears to have taken her teaching certificate at Georgetown College in 1945 at the age of nineteen – even more impressive as she seems not to have entered formal education until the age of twelve. She then worked for UNICEF on a child nutrition program, teaching impoverished communities about child development and health. In 1951 at the age of twenty-six she was selected from teachers across the Caribbean for an educational scholarship which saw her undertake a post-grauate thesis on early years education and its role in child development. She developed a lifelong interest in the impact of culture and ethnicity on child rearing and development. Eventually she became an expert on the then emerging field of attachment theory, applying Piaget's idioms to BAME children, which made her a pioneer in the field of ethno-psychology.

By 1953 she was working in London schools, teaching the Windrush children, whose parents were pursuing a similar immigrant dream but often in more chastened circumstances.

Despite being the graduate of a colonial scholarship for educators, when she first approached London boroughs looking to work as a teacher, she was told that her qualifications were not recognized. Undeterred she worked her way up from the bottom, undertaking additional quali-fications at night while bringing up two small children; she had by now married imminent black scientist Patrick Gilroy.

She is often cited as Britain's first black head-teacher and is frequently mistaken for Yvonne Connelly, who also became a headteacher with the Inner London Education Authority in the post-immigration period. However, in truth Beryl Gilroy was more of a writer and independent educator than a public servant. In writing *Black Teacher* she took a defiant stance against the race-politics in post-colonial institutions including schools.

Turned down by many publishers, her fictious black teacher is really an amalgam of all highly educated Caribbean women trying to plough the choppy fields of race prejudice in public sector workplaces.

Although she briefly become the head of a school in Kilburn, it was her writing, whilst homeschooling her children, that sets her apart. Her works of fiction, were somewhat overlooked, and ranged from the adult fiction of *Frangipani House* to the teen offerings of *Boy Sandwich*. Compared to V S Naipaul, or even her son Professor Paul Gilroy, commercial success as a writer eluded her.

However, the beauty of Beryl was that she was a polymath and entirely ahead of her time. She typified that most Caribbean of concepts in being the ultimate 'can-do-woman', if there was a job, she would say I can do it, if there was a story to tell she would say 'I can tell it'.

When she died of a heart attack in 2001 at age 76, Roxann Bradshaw was present at the 4th annual Caribbean Women Writers Association. She states 'there was not a dry eye in the house' when it was announced that keynote speaker Dr Gilroy had passed.

9 June
The fire last time: Ada Wright and the Scottsboro Nine

On March 25, 1931, nine young black men – Haywood Patterson, Clarence Norris, Charlie Weems, Andy and Roy Wright, Olin Montgomery, Ozie Powell, Willie Roberson, and Eugene Williams – were arrested for raping two white women on a train in Paint Rock, Alabama. The teenagers were taken to Scottsboro, Alabama where all but one, Roy Wright aged just thirteen, were tried, convicted, and sentenced to death.

The Scottsboro Nine's case galvanized an international movement organised by the Communist Party and the Labor Defense League. At the heart of this movement was Ada Wright, mother of Andy and Roy.

Ada was struggling to survive on wages of five dollars a week so, like thousands of others during the Great Depression, she allowed her sons Andy, nineteen, and Roy, twelve, to leave home to look for work.

Ada had never before left rural Tennessee, but now her sons were facing the electric chair, she faced down racist sneers and abuse to tour the US and Europe fighting for justice.

There were demonstrations for the Scottsboro Nine at US embassies in cities across Europe. In June 1931 protestors smashed windows at the US embassy in Berlin. In London, communists organised among the black and Asian dock workers in East London and black organisations. In February 1932, 2,000 marched from the Thames to Hyde Park, and in April supporters marched from Poplar and Bermondsey to the US embassy. Ada spoke at public meetings in Greenwich and in Willesden, where the crowd was estimated at five hundred. Crowds also greeted Ada in Bristol and Dundee, where they sang the 'Internationale'. She spoke at meetings in Kirkcaldy, Lockerbie, Springburn, Glasgow, and Manchester.

Communist leader Shapurji Saklatvala addressed Ada's farewell at Shoreditch church, saying, 'The British workers have shown by their reception to Mrs Wright that they have broken down the barriers dividing them from the negro races'. A thousand marchers accompanied her to Liverpool Street Station when she left for Scandinavia where 10,000 people demonstrated in Copenhagen.

Ada was arrested in Kladno, Czechoslovakia, on suspicion of spreading communist propaganda. She spent three nights in a cell before she was expelled from the country.

Ada ended the tour in Moscow and in Red Square, tens of thousands of workers crowded the streets with banners, calling for freedom for the sons of Ada Wright.

Ada gave interviews to *The Woman Worker*, a magazine published by the American Communist Party. In August 1934 *The Woman Worker* featured an article titled 'Think of Them' with the faces of four of the Scottsboro accused. Ada wrote an article in which she described the prison conditions the young men experienced, the lack of food and their mistreatment at the hands of guards.

The case went to the US Supreme Court in 1937, and the lives of the nine were saved, though it was almost twenty years before the last defendant was freed from prison.

The trial of the Scottsboro Nine is one of the high points of American radicalism, when a mass movement of blacks and whites – led by Communists – successfully beat the racist Jim Crow legal system.

10 June
Black Britain rising: Claudia Vera Jones (1915-1964)

Claudia Cumberbatch was born in 1915 in Port-of-Spain, Trinidad, which was then a British colony. Her family emigrated to New York City in 1922. Her mother, who worked in a garment factory, died in 1927.
As a student, Claudia joined the campaign to save the lives of the Scottsboro Nine, who were falsely accused of raping two white women in Alabama. The young African-American men only escaped execution because of the campaign by the Communist Party.
Claudia was a brilliant student, but she had to take on unskilled jobs in laundries, factories and shops in order to survive. In 1932, at the age of seventeen, she contracted tuberculosis which was to shorten her life.
She became deeply involved with left politics and joined the Young Communist League in 1936. She became a staff writer for the *Daily Worker*, and a Communist Party organiser in Harlem. In the early 1940s, Claudia served on the National Council of the YCL, and the editorial board of the *Weekly Review*. In 1945, she was appointed 'Negro Affairs' editor of the *Daily Worker* and joined the Communist Party's National Committee. In 1950, Claudia talked about 'the special discrimination facing Negro women as women, as workers and as Negroes'.
During the MacCarthyite witch hunts the FBI discovered that Claudia had been denied US citizenship. She was arrested on immigration charges in 1948 and held at the notorious Ellis Island detention facility. A campaign was launched that succeeded in postponing her deportation.
In 1951, Claudia was charged with violating the

Notting Hill
Carnival 2018

Smith Act, which outlawed support for over-
throwing the US government. After a national
campaign, she was again released but was forced
to leave the US and came to live in Britain where
she campaigned against racism in housing,
education and employment. Claudia launched the

anti-racist, anti-imperialist *West
Indian Gazette,* which was based
in Brixton. In August 1958, race
riots broke out in Notting Hill.
In response Claudia initiated the
famous Notting Hill Caribbean
Carnival.

Claudia died in December 1964, aged 49. She
was buried in Highgate cemetery near Karl Marx.
A message from Paul Robeson was read at her
funeral: 'She was a vigorous and courageous
leader of the Communist Party of the United
States, and was very active in the work for the
unity of white and coloured peoples and for
dignity and equality, especially for the Negro
people and for women.'

11 June
Why the statues must fall: Wambui Otieno and the Mau Mau Uprising (1936-2011)

Wambui was born in Kiambu District in southern Kikuyuland in 1936 to a well-off family of landowners. Her father, Tiras Waiyaki Wantoni, was a police inspector and her three elder brothers were educated in Britain. Wambui was the great granddaughter of Waiyaki wa Hinga, a Kikuyu leader who was arrested in 1892 by officials of the Imperial British East Africa Company. He died soon after the arrest. Wambui later wrote that he was buried alive for opposing the violent seizure of Kikuyu land.

During the Mau Mau rebellion of 1952-60, members of the Kikuyu tribe were detained in concentration camps, where they were systematically tortured and sexually assaulted. Up to 100,000 rebels died. The Kenya Human Rights Commission estimated 90,000 Kenyans were killed or maimed and 160,000 detained during the uprising. In 1952, while at secondary school, Wambui swore an oath of allegiance to Mau Mau and in 1954 she left home to join the Mau Mau insurgency in Nairobi.

Wambui spied on the British and mobilised women and domestic staff to obtain arms. She campaigned to eradicate the 'colour bar' in Nairobi, which designated separate areas in public spaces for Europeans, Asians and Africans. She was arrested several times and served with orders excluding her from Nairobi, which she flouted. Wambui had three children with her fiancé, who she was unable to marry because of family opposition.

After Mau Mau forces had been defeated, she became involved in trade union activities. She was arrested in July 1960 for mobilising women for strikes and riots and detained in a camp in Lamu until January 1961. In the camp she was raped and impregnated by a British prison officer. After her release from detention, Wambui became active in a series of Kenyan political parties including the Kiama Kia Muingi, an organisation that was a successor to Mau Mau.

She was one of the first women to run for political office in postcolonial Kenya as a KANU candidate in 1969 and stood again in 1974, although she was unsuccessful. She served as an official in a number of Kenyan and international Women's organisations.

It was not until 2013, that Mau Mau rebels who were raped, castrated and beaten by British troops were awarded £14 million compensation – but there was no apology.

Mau Mau fighters in Scout Uniforms, c. 1963.

13 June
Why the statues must fall: Pritilata Waddedar (1911 -1932)

Pritilata was born to a middle-class Vaidya
(Baidya) family in Dhalghat village in Patiya
Upazila, Chittagong now in Bangladesh.
She graduated from Dr Khastagir's Government
Girls' School in 1928 and in 1929 she was admitted
to the Eden College, Dhaka, where she became
a top student. Pritilata then went to Calcutta,
now Kolkata, to attend the Bethune College. She
graduated in philosophy and was awarded a
distinction. However, her degree was withheld by
British authorities for political reasons.
Pritilata returned to Chittagong to take up the job
of headmistress at an English secondary school
where she joined the Indian independence movement against British colonialism. One man, Binod
Bihari Chowdhury, objected to women joining
the group, but Pritalata argued her case and was
allowed to join. 'Pritilata was young and coura-
geous. She would work with a lot of zeal and was
determined to drive the British away,' Chowdhury
later acknowledged.
Pritilata took part in many raids on British
targets, such as the Telephone & Telegraph
offices. In 1932, the group planned an attack on
the Pahartali European Club, whose sign read
'Dogs and Indians not allowed'. Pritilata was the
leader of the attack and prepared herself with
arms training.
On 23 September 1932, Pritilata dressed herself
as a Punjabi man and led a group of fifteen
revolu-tionaries to torch the club. Police officers
inside the club started shooting and Pritilata
received a bullet wound. Pritilata was trapped by
the British police and swallowed cyanide to avoid
getting arrested. She was twenty-one years old.
In 2012, the University of Calcutta posthumously
awarded Pritilata the degree the British had
denied her.

14 June: Suggested by my friend and fellow educator Farida Haque:
Why the Statues Must Fall: Leela Roy (Bengali: নীলা রায়)
(1900-1970)

Leela was born into an upper middle-class Bengali Hindu Kayastha family in Sylhet in Bengal and educated at the Bethune College in Calcutta, graduating with a gold medal in English. Leela had to fight with university authorities to become the first woman admitted to the University of Dhaka. She threw herself into social work and education for girls, starting several girls' schools in Dhaka. In 1921 during the Bengal floods, Leela, who was then a student at Dhaka University, was instrumental in forming the Dhaka Women's Committee to organise flood relief. In 1931, she began publishing *Jayasree*, the first magazine edited, managed, and written by women writers.

Leela formed a rebel organisation called Deepali Sangha in Dhaka at the end of 1923. She took part in the Civil Disobedience Movement and was imprisoned for six years. In 1938, she was nominated to the National Planning Committee of the Congress. She married Anil Chandra Roy in the same year.

In 1942, when the Quit India Movement was at its height, both she and her husband were ar-rested and her magazine was shut down. On her release from prison in 1946, she was elected to the Constituent Assembly of India.

During the partition violence, she met Gandhi in Noakhali, where she had opened a relief center and helped hundreds of women. After the Partition of India, she ran homes in Calcutta for destitute women and helped refugees from East Bengal. Leela founded Jatiya Mahila Sanghati, a women's organisation in West Bengal 1947. She continued to be active during the 1960s and died in June 1970.

17 June
Emma Tenayuca (1916-1999)

Emma Tenayuca grew up in a Mexican Comanche family of eleven and was raised by her grandparents. The family were hit hard by the Depression, and Emma became a labour activist before graduating from Brackenridge High School in San Antonio.

Emma was first arrested aged sixteen, in 1933, when she joined a picket line of workers striking against the Finck Cigar Company. After high school, she worked as an elevator operator, but she continued her union activism. She founded two international ladies' garment workers unions and was involved in both the Worker's Alliance of America and Woman's League for Peace and Freedom.

She organised a protest over the beating of Mexican migrants by United States Border Patrol agents. She was arrested twice, once for 'disturbing the peace' during a nonviolent protest, and again for her leadership role in a strike in 1938. 'I was arrested a number of times. I don't think that I felt exactly fearful. I never thought in terms of fear. I thought in terms of justice', Emma later recalled.

Emma was instrumental in one of the most famous conflicts of Texas labour history – the 1938 San Antonio pecan shellers strike at the Southern Pecan Shelling Company. During the strike, thousands of workers at over 130 plants protested against a wage reduction. Mexicana and Chicana workers who picketed were gassed, arrested, and jailed. The strike ended after 37 days and in October, the National Labor Relations Act raised their wages.

Emma joined the Communist Party in 1936. In 1937, she was due to speak at a Communist Party meeting at the Municipal Auditorium. A crowd of 5,000 attacked the auditorium with bricks and

Emma, centre, with strikers at Southern Pecan Shelling Company

rocks, 'huntin' communists'. Emma escaped from the mob, but she was blacklisted and forced to move out of San Antonio
In 1938 she married organizer Homer Brooks and took a college degree. She divorced Brooks in 1941 and left her hometown in order to attend San Francisco State College, where she majored in education. She later earned a master's in education from Our Lady of the Lake University in San Antonio. Emma went on to teach in Harlandale School District until her retirement in 1982. Emma Tenayuca developed Alzheimer's disease and died on 23 July, 1999.

19 June
America rising: Charlene Alexander Mitchell (1930-)

Born in Cincinnati, Ohio in 1930, Charlene migrated with her working-class family to Chicago. During World War II, she grew up in the Frances Cabrini Housing Rowhouses and took classes at nearby Moody Bible Institutes. When she was just seven, Charlene's mother was so ill that Charlene had to take food to her labour-activist father, who was serving a prison sentence. After several terrifying bus transfers, she arrived late and had to argue with guards to be allowed to see her dad and to stop the guards taking the food she had bought from home. She later recalled, 'I probably have been trying to be an organiser most of my life'.

In 1943, at the age of thirteen, Charlene joined black and white teenagers in picketing segregated theatres and bowling allies. She joined the American Youth for Democracy which staged sit-ins in 'whites-only' areas.

Charlene joined the Communist Party in 1946 aged sixteen. In 1955, she moved to Los Angeles and in 1957, at the age of twenty-seven, she became the youngest person ever elected to the Communist Party's National Committee. For the next thirty years, she remained a high ranking Communist Party official.

In 1967 she founded the Che-Lumumba Club, an all-black, CPUsA club in Los Angeles through which Angela Davis joined the CP. Charlene became Angela's mentor and her close friend. Charlene was the executive director of the National United Committee to Free Angela Davis, helping to forge a broad Free Angela Davis movement which linked Davis's case to demands for social justice, black liberation, women's rights, free speech, peace, and Third World liberation. Charlene recalled visiting London in 1960 and meeting Claudia Jones and Yusuf Dadoo, an

Indian member of the Communist Party and a member of the Indian Congress of South Africa: 'So to me, Africa opened its doors, to me, more as part of the movement and solidarity with us as we were with them. And I kind of always saw that as an equal thing, because I would learn so much from it.'

Charlene was one of the Communist Party's most influential leaders during the 1950s and 1960s, developing the party's links with African-American labour activists and pushing for the party to engage with Third World liberation movements. Charlene travelled widely and met various African liberation movement leaders, most notably Amilcar Cabral of the African Party for the Liberation of Guinea-Bissau and Cape Verde.

Charlene was the CP candidate in the US Presidential Election of 1968, the first African-American woman to run for President of the US. In 1988, she ran as an Independent Progressive for US Senator from New York against the incumbent Daniel Patrick Moynihan, but he was re-elected by a large margin. As of 2006, Mitchell was active in the Committees of Correspondence for Democracy and Socialism (CCDS), an independent offshoot of the Communist Party.

20 June
Rebellious Mother and Daughter of History: Esther Georgia Irving Cooper (1881-1970) Esther Cooper Jackson (1917 -)

Esther was born in Cleveland, Ohio. Her parents were former slaves. Esther taught English and she founded and became president of the Arlington County branch of the National Association for the Advancement of Colored People. In 1942, she joined the executive board of the Virginia State Conference of the NAACP, which challenged racial inequalities in the county's high schools. This culminated in Carter

v. School Board of Arlington County, when courts ruled that segregated schools constituted unlawful racial discrimination. Esther senior was also a member of the Southern Conference for Human Welfare. She regis-tered voters and campaigned to end voting poll taxes. Esther married George Posea Cooper in 1913, and they had three daughters. one of whom was named Esther Cooper.

Esther junior attended segregated schools but went on to study at Oberlin College and to be awarded a master's degree in sociology from Fisk University in 1940. Her 1940 thesis was called *The Negro Woman Domestic Worker in Relation to Trade Unionism.*

She joined the Southern Negro Youth Congress, where she met her future husband James Jackson, a Communist and trade union activist. Together, they fought to desegregate transport and promote the rights of blacks and poor whites. In 1942, twenty-three-year-old Esther delivered the opening address of the Fifth All-Southern Negro Youth Conference in Alabama. She focused special attention on black women, who were central to 'the preservation of democracy in the world.' Esther believed that black women's freedom was critical to defeating Jim Crow, fascism, and colonialism.

In 1952, she moved to New York City and joined the American Communist party. In 1961, she became editor of *Freedomways*, the central theoretical journal of the 20th century black arts and intellectual movement in the US. Esther called the publication, 'a tool for the libera-tion of our people.'

The Jacksons faced persecution during the McCarthy years but continued to be active in the Civil Rights Movement. Esther played an important role in the Free Angela Davis

Campaign and never stopped campaigning for social change. James Jackson died in 2007 aged 92. Esther celebrated her 101 birthday and, as far as I can dis-cover, is still alive.

Poem:
Beulah (Beah) Richards A Black woman speaks: of white womanhood, of white supremacy, of peace: a poem (1951)

 Beulah was an actress and writer. She wrote, *A Black Woman Speaks*, a collection of fourteen poems, in which she points out how, while white women were enslaved, they played a role in oppressing women of colour. From the 1930s to the late 1950s, Beulah was a member and or-ganizer with the Communist Party USA in Los Angeles after befriending artist Paul Robeson. She is among the black women who 'actively participated in movements affiliated with the CPUSA' between the 1917 Bolshevik Revolution and the 1950s. She was later a sponsor of the National United Committee to Free Angela Davis.

A Black Woman Speaks

It is right that I a woman black, should speak of white womanhood. my fathers my brothers my husbands my sons die for it: because of it. and their blood chilled in electric chairs, stopped by hangman's noose, cooked by lynch mobs' fire, spilled by white supremacist mad desire to kill give me that right
...

Death for me and worse than death for you. What will you do? Will you fight with me? White supremacy is your enemy and mine. So be careful when you talk with me. Remind me not of my slavery, I know it will but rather tell me of your own. Remember, you have never known me. You've been busy seeing me as white supremacist would have me be, and I will be myself. Free! My aim is full equality. I would usurp their plan! Justice peace and plenty for every man, woman and child who walks the earth. This is my fight! If you will fight with me then take my hand and the hand of Rosa Ingram, and Rosalee McGee, and as we set about our plan let our Wholehearted fight be: PEACE IN A WORLD WHERE THERE IS EQUALITY.

You can read the whole poem here:
http://httpjournalsaolcomjenjer6steph.blogspot.com/2014/04/a-black-women-speaks.html

21 June Today's post has been written by the indefatigable housing campaigner, Glyn Robbins: **Shirley Chisholm** (1924-2005)

Shirley Chisholm was a trail-blazer for US politicians like Alexandria Ocasio-Cortez. She was the first black woman elected to Congress, returned by the people of her native workingclass Brooklyn neighbourhood in 1968. Four years later, she became the first black woman to run for the US Presidency. Her candidacy for the Democratic Party nomination was a long-shot, but as she said, 'someone had to go first' and it represented a significant moment in the fight for equality that continues today in the shape of #BlackLivesMatter. Shirley Chisholm was, first and last, a teacher. The daughter of poor Caribbean immigrants to the US, she was sent to live with her grandmother in Barbados as a young child, where she excelled academically. After returning to the country of her birth, Chisholm started a successful career in education, but also developed an interest in politics, partly inherited from her father, a labourer and follower of Marcus Garvey.

Chisholm resisted playing the establishment political game. Her autobiography is called *Unbought and Unbossed*. She faced institutional racism and sexism in Congress, recalling sitting on her own in the Capital Hill dining room and being allocated to committees with little influence. When she sought the Democratic Party's nomination for President, she came under pressure to withdraw for more moderate candidates. Her campaign was snuffed out by the party machine, but Chisholm continued to champion progressive causes like Palestinian and abortion rights and opposition to apartheid South Africa and the Vietnam War. This marked her out as an enemy to the corrupt Nixon regime, who smeared her with false accusations.

■ The actress Viola Davis is planning a biopic of the woman who said 'racism is invisible because it's so normal.'

23 June
Bina Das (1911–1986)

Bina was an Indian revolutionary and nationalist from West Bengal. She was the daughter of
a well known Brahmo teacher, Beni Madhab
Das and a social worker, Sarala Devi. Her elder
sister Kalyani Das (Bhattacharyee) was also a
freedom fighter.
Bina was a student of St. John's Diocesan
Girls' Higher Secondary School. She became a
member of Chhatri Sangha, a semi-revolutionary
organisation for women in Kolkata. On 6
February, 1932, she attempted to assassinate
the Bengal Governor Stanley Jackson, in the
Convocation Hall of the University of Calcutta.
The revolver was supplied by another freedom
fighter Kamala Das Gupta. Bina fired five shots
but failed to kill the Governor. She was sentenced
to nine years in prison.
After her early release in 1939, Bina joined the
Congress party. In 1942, she participated in
the Quit India movement and was imprisoned
again from 1942-45. From 1946-47, she was a
member of the Bengal Provincial Legislative
Assembly and from 1947-51 she was a member of
the West Bengal Legislative Assembly. In 1947,
she married Jatish Chandra Bhaumik, an Indian
independence movement activist.
Her sister edited Kalyani Bhattacharjee a book
called *Bengal Speaks*, published in 1944, and
dedicated it to her. She won the Padma Shri
award in 1960 for her social work. In 2012, she
and Pritilata Waddedar* were both conferred
their certificates of merit posthumously.
After the death of her husband, Bina led a lonely
life in Rishikesh and died in anonymity. Her body
was recovered from the roadside on 26 December
1986. It took police a month to identity her.

* Pritilata Waddedar is the subject of a previous section

25 June
Black America rising: Shirley Graham Du Bois (1896-1977)

Lola Shirley Graham Jr. was born in Indianapolis, Indiana, in 1896, one of six children. Her father was a minister in the African Methodist Episcopal. In June 1915, Shirley graduated from Lewis and Clark High School in Spokane, Washington.

She married her first husband, Shadrach T McCants, in 1921. Their son Robert was born in 1923, followed by David in 1925. In 1926, Shirley moved to Paris, France, to study music composition at the Sorbonne to provide a better life for her children.

In 1931, Shirley entered Oberlin College and was awarded her BA. In 1932, she composed an opera, *Tom Tom: An Epic of Music and the Negro*. She used music and dance to express the story of Africans' journey to the North American colonies, through slavery and to freedom. The opera attracted 10,000 people to its premiere at the Cleveland Stadium.

Shirley and Shadrach divorced in 1927. In 1934, she went on to do graduate work in music, completing a master's degree in 1935. In 1936, Shirley was appointed director of the Chicago Negro Unit of the Federal Theater Project.

In the late 1940s, Shirley became a member of Sojourners for Truth and Justice – an African-American organisation working for global women's liberation. She also joined the American Communist Party and became a key organiser in the Rosa Lee Ingram campaign. Rosa was an African-American sharecropper and widowed mother of twelve. In 1948, Rosa and her two teenage sons were sentenced to the electric chair after a fight with a white neighbour who had sexually harassed Rosa. He was not charged with any offence. The death sentence was handed down by an all-white jury and scheduled to take place less than three weeks later, but the country erupted in protests against the trial, led by the Sojourners for Truth and Justice. The Ingram family's sentences were commuted to life in April 1948. Further campaigning saw them released ten years later.

Shirley turned to decolonising literature by writing biographies of leading African-American and world leaders such as Paul Robeson, Kwame Nkrumah, Phillis Wheatley, and Booker T Wash-ington aimed at young readers. She won a prize for *There Once Was a Slave* (1947), a novel about Frederick Douglass.

In 1951, she married the great activist WEB Du Bois, the second marriage for both. They later emigrated to Ghana, where he died in 1963. She met Malcolm X in Ghana in 1964. In 1967, Ghanaian president, Kwame Nkrumah, was overthrown and Shirley moved first to Egypt and then to Tanzania. Shirley Graham Du Bois died of breast cancer on March 27, 1977, aged 80, in Beijing, China.

W E B Du Bois and Shirley Graham Du Bois on board the S S *Liberté*, August 1958

27 June
Katharine Chidley and the English Revolution

Katherine Chidley was born around 1598. In 1616 she married Daniel Chidley, a tailor of Shrewsbury. She gave birth to eight children. In 1626 she and her husband were prosecuted for non-attendance at church. She was also reported for refusing 'to come to be churched after childbirth'.

The family moved to London and mixed with radicals. Katherine become a preacher in Stepney, east London. She also began writing religious pamphlets which challenged the authority of the church hierarchy, suggesting that the humblest members of society, were better qualified to create churches than 'ill-meaning priests'. She argued that 'a husband had no more right to control his wife's conscience than the magistrate had to control his'.

In January 1642, civil broke out between parliament and royalist forces led by Charles I. Katherine associated with Levellers, the radical wing of the parliamentary side who demanded democracy, and end to censorship, the abolition of the monarchy and the House of Lords and an end to taxation of the poor.

In February 1649, Leveller leader John Lilburne was arrested for protesting against Cromwell's military government. Katherine organised Britain's first ever all-woman petition of parliament with 10,000 signatures demanding Lilburne's release. Women protested outside parliament and faced down soldiers, who pointed muskets at them, to get the petition presented to the House of Commons on 25 April, 1649. Parliament's response was to tell the women, 'The matter you petition about is of an higher concernment then you understand therefore you are desired to goe home, and looke after your owne businesses, and meddle with your housewifery.'

Daniel Chidley died in 1649 and Katherine Chiley took over her his haberdashery business.

In 1653 John Lilburne was again on trial, this time for his life. Twelve women, led by Katherine, again confronted Parliament with a petition signed by 6,000 women. They boldly knocked on the door but were sent away. An MP told them that parliament could not recognise their petition, 'they being women and many of them wives, so that the Law tooke no notice of them'. However, John Lilburne was later acquitted to popular rejoicing. This was the last heard of Katherine, although her son Samuel continued her fight for democracy.

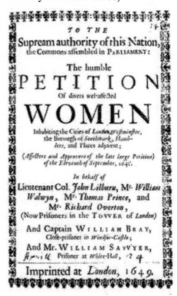

TO THE Supream authority of this Nation, the Commons assembled in PARLIAMENT:

The humble

PETITION

Of divers wel-affected

WOMEN

Inhabiting the Cities of London, Westminster, the Borough of Southwark, Hamblets, and Places adjacent;

(Affecters and Approvers of the late large Petition of the Eleventh of September, 1648.

In behalf of

Lieutenant Col. John Lilburn, Mr. William Walwyn, Mr. Thomas Prince, and Mr. Richard Overton, (Now Prisoners in the TOWER of London)

And Captain WILLIAM BRAY, Close-prisoner in Windsor-Castle;

And Mr. WILLIAM SAWYER, Prisoner at White-Hall,

Imprinted at London, 1649.

4 July
The French Revolution: Théroigne de Méricourt (1762–1817)

Théroigne was born in Marcourt, Rendeux. Her mother died after giving birth, and she was sent to live with her aunt in Liége. She left after being forced to work as a servant.

In 1789, Théroigne became swept up in the early stirrings of the Revolution. She attended meetings of the National Assembly, and helped to set up the Society of Friends of the Law, which encouraged revolutionary activity in the provinces. Théroigne was a passionate advocate of women's rights, arguing that, 'Women have the same natural rights as men, so that, as a consequence, it is supremely unjust that we have not the same rights in society'. The royalist press attacked Théroigne as a 'patriots' whore' who was 'ever to be found where the unrest was greatest'. In May 1790, Théroigne was captured by Austrian Troops. She was interrogated and abused but eventually released due to her bad health. Théroigne returned to Paris in January 1792 to a hero's welcome. She spoke at the Jacobin Club, and was praised as 'one of the first Amazons of liberty'. She was awarded a civic crown for her courage during the overthrow of the monarchy. Théroigne campaigned for women to be armed: 'Frenchwomen ... let us raise ourselves to the height of our destinies; let us break our chains!' In early 1793 she allied herself with the Girondins who were then opponents of the radical Jacobins. On 15 May Théroigne was delivering a speech when she was attacked by a group of women Jacobins and was rescued by Jean-Paul Marat. Théroigne's behavior became erratic, and on 20 September 1794 she was certified insane and put into an asylum. She was sent to La Salpêtrière Hospital in 1807, where she lived for ten years, intermittently lucid and speaking constantly about the Revolution. Following a short illness, she died there on 9 June, 1817.

5 July
Why the statues must fall: Sarah 'Sally' Hemings

Thomas Jefferson was an American statesman, diplomat, lawyer, architect, philosopher, Founding Father and third president of the United States from 1801 to 1809. The principal author of the Declaration of Independence, Jefferson was a proponent of democracy, republicanism, and individual rights.

But Sally Hemings was his slave. Jefferson's wife Martha inherited Sally, her five siblings and her mother, Betty, from her father, John Wayles. Wayles was also the father of Betty's children. The slaves were Martha's half sisters and brothers.

In 1787 Sally, then aged fourteen, accompanied Jefferson's younger daughter Mary 'Polly' to London and then to Paris, where the widowed Jefferson was serving as the US Minister to France. During Sally's two years in Paris, Jefferson, then aged 44, began to rape her. Her son later suggested that Sally only agreed to return to the US with Jefferson on condition the child she was carrying would be freed. Sally herself remained enslaved in Jefferson's house until his death. She lived in basement rooms under his mansion.

Jefferson has been proved to be the father of Sally's six children (four of whom survived into adulthood). The children lived in Jefferson's house as slaves and were trained as artisans but Jefferson did free all of Sally's surviving children as they came of age.

After Jefferson's death, Sally was 'given her time' by his daughter in an informal granting of freedom. She lived her last nine years with her two younger sons in Charlottesville, Virginia. She saw a grandchild born in the house her sons owned.

11 July: Inspired by the Tower Hamlets Unison Strike:
The Chocolate Women's Strike, East London, 1890

Clementina Black, secretary of the Women's Trade Union League, organised a meeting for the young women working at Messrs Allen's chocolate factory on 10 July, 1890: 'Twelve girls came, and their dread of being followed, watched and subsequently discharged was pitiful.'

The next day, the Women's League sent Miss James, an organiser and former confectionary worker, to leaflet the workers. They surrounded her, telling her that they were 'out' and asking anxiously, 'What shall we do?' Miss James led them to the office of the Women's Trade Union Association, 128 Mile End Road.

A young woman had fallen at work and was fined. She refused to pay and was threatened with the sack. The other women stopped work and demanded her reinstatement and raised other grievances. They were forbidden to leave the factory in the dinner hour, forbidden to eat between eight and one, and were subject to fines. A meeting was held at Mile End Liberal and Radical Club at which a committee was elected and all those present joined the union.

The following Monday morning, union organiser John Burns and Miss James were at the factory gates before 8am, and picketing began. Solidarity came from dockers at Woolwich Arsenal, who were lining up to put money in a bucket.

By Wednesday, Allen agreed to meet the women. They demanded reinstatement for the young woman, a right to leave the factory at lunchtime, an end to fines, and a promise of no punishment for those who had joined the union.

Allen agreed to all the demands except the abolition of fines for lateness, which he agreed to reduce. An agreement was finally signed on 22 July, and work at the chocolate factory resumed.

12 July: Inspired by the Tower Hamlets Unison Strike:
The Atlanta Laundresses Strike, 1881

L ess than two decades after the Emancipation of the Slaves Act was passed, Atlanta had only primitive water and sewer systems. In the 1880s, some 98 percent of the city's black working women were domestic workers and most were laundresses. Laundry work was the most difficult of domestic jobs, with long hours and low pay. In July 1881, twenty laundresses met to form a trade organisation, the Washing Society. They demanded higher pay, autonomy over their work and to establish a uniform rate at $1 per dozen pounds of wash. They held a mass meeting and called a strike to win higher pay at the uniform rate. The Washing Society, organised door-to-door canvassing to recruit members and urged laundresses to join the strike. They also involved white laundresses, who were less than 2 percent of laundresses in Atlanta – an extraordinary sign of interracial solidarity. In three weeks, the Washing Society grew from 20 to 3,000 strikers. By August, municipal authorities had begun arresting strikers and fining members. The City Council proposed that members of any washerwoman's organization pay an annual fee of $25, several months of wages. The strikers responded with a letter to the mayor, agreeing to pay the fees rather than be defeated. The striking laundresses inspired other domestic workers. Cooks, maids and nurses began demanding higher wages. Hotel workers also went on strike. The following week, the City Council rejected the proposed fees. The laundresses had won. The strike not only raised wages, more importantly, it established black women workers as central to the South's economy. The white establishment was forced to acknowledge that black women workers, who were former slaves, were not invisible but were workers with collective power.

18 July
'The Uprising of the 20,000', New York, 1909

On 23 November, 1909, more than twenty thousand Yiddish-speaking immigrants, mostly young women in their teens and early twenties, launched an eleven-week general strike in New York's shirtwaist industry.

Workers shared common grievances over wages, hours, workplace safety, and workplace indignities suffered specifically by women, such as unwanted sexual advances.

The young strikers faced opposition from the manufacturers, the police, and the courts. Bosses hired thugs to abuse strikers, policemen arrested them on trumped-up charges of assault and courts fined them and sentenced them to the workhouse.

Members of the Women's Trade Union League monitored the picket lines and raised funds. The Forverts, the United Hebrew Trades, the Arbeter-ring (Workmen's Circle), and the Socialist Party all provided support.

By November, Local 25 had no strike funds left but rather than give in, Local 25's fifteen-member executive committee (six of whom were women

and all socialists) called for a general strike to
shut down the shirtwaist industry.

On 22 November, thousands of young women
packed into a hall to discuss the strike call. For
two hours, they heard speakers urging caution.
Then Clara Lemlich Shavelson demanded the
floor. Speaking Yiddish, she electrified the crowd:
'I am a working girl, one of those who are on
strike against intolerable conditions. I am tired of
listening to speakers who talk in general terms.
What we are here to decide is whether we shall or
shall not strike. I offer a resolution that a general
strike be declared now.' The crowd unanimously
pledged support for the general strike.

The following morning, approximately 15,000
shirtwaist workers took to the streets. By evening,
the number swelled to more than 20,000, 90
percent of whom were Jewish and 70 percent
women.

Clara Lemlich suffered six broken ribs and was
arrested a total of seventeen times. The strikers –
malnourished and poorly clad handed out leaflets,

raised funds, distributed strike
benefits and organised meetings.
The general strike was called off
on 15 February, 1910. The uprising
achieved significant gains. Most
workshops granted a 52-hour
week, at least four paid holidays,
no discrimination against union
loyalists, no charges for tools and
materials and negotiation of wages.

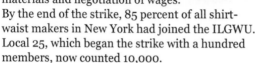

By the end of the strike, 85 percent of all shirtwaist makers in New York had joined the ILGWU.
Local 25, which began the strike with a hundred
members, now counted 10,000.

Inspired by the shirtwaist makers, 60,000 cloak
makers – men, this time – launched the Great
Revolt in the summer of 1910.

After five years of unrest, the 'needle trades'
emerged as one of the best organised in the
United States.

19 July: Yesterday's post was about the Uprising of the 20,000. Todays is about one of the leaders of that uprising – **Clara Lemlich** (1886-1982)

Clara was born 28 March, 1886, in the Ukrainian city of Gorodok, to a Jewish family. Clara wrote letters for illiterate neighbours to raise money for her books. A neighbour introduced her to revolutionary literature, and Clara became a committed socialist. She immigrated to the United States with her family in 1903, following a pogrom in Kishinev. Clara found a job in the garment industry in New York. She became involved in the International Ladies' Garment Workers' Union and was elected to the executive board of Local 25 of the ILGWU. On 22 November, 1909, Clara attended a mass

meeting held at Cooper Union to rally support for striking shirtwaist workers. For two hours the leading figures of the American labour movement held forth. Clara demanded to speak. Lifted onto the platform, she said: 'I have listened to all the speakers, and I have no further patience for talk. I am a working girl, one of those striking against intolerable conditions. I am tired of listening to speakers who talk in generali-ties. What we are here for is to decide whether or not to strike. I make a motion that we go out in a general strike.'

The crowd voted for a general strike.

Approximately 20,000 out of the 32,000 workers in the shirtwaist trade walked out in the next two days in what became known as the 'Uprising of the 20,000'. Clara spoke at rallies until she lost her voice and returned to the picket lines with six broken ribs after being beaten by police.

The strike lasted until 10 February, 1910 and succeeded in winning union contracts at almost every shop.

Blacklisted from the industry, Clara devoted

herself to the campaign for women's suffrage.
Clara fell out with the middle-class suffrage leaders and set up the Wage Earner's Suffrage League.
Clara continued her suffrage activities for the
Women's Trade Union League. Clara married Joe
Shavelson in 1913. She had five children.
In 1926, she joined the Communist Party and
began organising housewives in the east side.
Clara organised The United Council of Working
Class Housewives, which organised boycotts,
stopped evictions raised money and organised
child care for strikers.
In 1929, Clara launched the United Council of
Working Class Women, which had nearly 50
branches in New York City. The Council led a
boycott of butcher shops to protest high meat
prices in 1935, using flying pickets to close more
than 4,000 butchers' shops in New York City.
The strike was based in the Jewish and African-
American communities. The Councils were
destroyed by the anti communist witch hunts of
the early 1950s.
Clara then became active in the Emma Lazarus
Federation of Jewish Women's Clubs, protesting
against nuclear weapons, and against the War in
Vietnam, stopping evictions and forging alliances
with Sojourners for Truth, an African-American
women's civil rights organization.
Clara remained an unwavering member of the
Communist Party, denouncing the trial and
execution of the Rosenbergs. Her passport was
revoked after a trip to the Soviet Union in 1951.
She moved to California to be near her children
in the 1960s, and entered the Jewish Home for
the Aged in Los Angeles, where she persuaded the
management to join in the United Farm Workers
boycott of grapes and lettuce. She died at the
home on 12 July, 1982, at aged 96.

23 August: Guest post from Sam Kirk
Hertha Marks Ayrton (1854 – 1923)

I t is a pleasure to tell the story of a scientist to which I have three affinities. Firstly she is a physicist, secondly she helped found an organisation that became the first trade union I joined as a science technician in the NHS, and thirdly she was an activist trying to make the world a better place.

Born Sarah Marks to Jewish parents, she showed great promise as a child. Due to family hardship after the death of her father, her education was funded by others.

As a woman scientist, she was not taken seriously by many institutions. She invented many things, but her most well-known achievements were the invention of a line divider used by engineers for scale diagrams, arcing in lamps and the Ayrton fan. If you've ever been to the 'flicks' but wondered why cinemas are sometimes called this because there is no flickering, you have Hertha Ayrton to thank. The lamps originally used in cinemas and street lights were unstable so caused flickering. Hertha redesigned them, stabilising the light source and getting rid of the flickering, but the name for cinemas continued.

Her work attracted the attention of other scientists and she was proposed by one male scientist to become a Fellow of the Royal Society in 1902, only given to top scientists then and now. However, married women were not admitted at the time. Two years after her rejection, she was allowed to read a paper to the Royal Society, becoming the first woman to do so. It took another twenty years for women to be allowed to become Fellows [sic] of the Royal Society!

She invented many other things. Her invention of a fan to clear poisonous gas from the trenches in the World War I was at first turned down, but later adopted and also used in mines.

A woman not afraid to speak out, after Marie
Curie's discovery of Radium was wrongly
attributed to Curie's husband, Ayrton engaged
with the media regarding the sexism: 'Errors are
notoriously hard to kill, but an error that ascribes
to a man what was actually the work of a woman
has more lives than a cat'. This had also happened
to Ayrton, despite the fact that her husband was
keen for her to get recognition for her work and
fully supported her. She and Marie Curie were
friends.

After Curie needed somewhere to rest, following
an operation on her kidney, and being pilloried
in the French press with sexist and racist abuse
for having a relationship with a man who, whilst
married, was separated from his wife and Curie
was a widow, Curie and her teenage daughters,
Irene and Eve, stayed with Hertha in 1912. Ayrton
taught Irene maths and it was through Irene that
Ayrton persuaded Marie Curie to sign the petition
against the imprisoning of suffragettes, something
that Curie was normally averse to.

The stay coincided with the most active time for
Hertha in the suffragette campaign (1911-1913) and
probably influenced the young Irene, who became
involved in politics later in life.

Joining the Women's Social and Political Union
(WPSU) in 1907, she got involved in a variety of
ways, attending the marches, looking after many
of the women (including Emily Pankhurst), when
they were released from prison after being force
fed during the tortuous cat and mouse episodes.

Like many other women, Hertha refused to fill in
the 1911 census. Instead she wrote on the paper:
'How can I answer all these questions if I have not
the intelligence to choose between two candidates
for parliament? I will not supply these particu-
lars until I have my rights as a citizen. Votes for
Women.'

She agreed to have WPSU money transferred
to her account to protect it from threatened
confiscation by the state.

A formidable woman, George Elliot allegedly based the character Mirah in her novel *Daniel Deronda* on Ayrton. Elliot along with others supported Ayrton to study at Girton College Cambridge, having no independent means. Like other women of the time, although completing her degree studies she was not allowed to be awarded her degree. A situation that didn't change until 1948!

Ayrton was also a founding member of National

Union of Scientific Workers, which later merged with another union becoming the Association of Scientific, Technical and Managerial Staffs (ASTMS).

Her daughter Barbara also joined her on WPSU marches and went on to become a Labour MP.

INDEX